BE

WISE

BE

WISE

DISCERN THE DIFFERENCE BETWEEN MAN'S KNOWLEDGE AND GOD'S WISDOM

NT COMMENTARY

1 CORINTHIANS

Warren W. Wiersbe

David C Cook
transforming lives together

BE WISE
Published by David C Cook
4050 Lee Vance View
Colorado Springs, CO 80918 U.S.A.

David C Cook Distribution Canada
55 Woodslee Avenue, Paris, Ontario, Canada N3L 3E5

David C Cook U.K., Kingsway Communications
Eastbourne, East Sussex BN23 6NT, England

The graphic circle C logo is a registered trademark of David C Cook.

Unless otherwise noted, all Scripture quotations are taken from the King James Version of the
Bible. (Public Domain.) Scripture quotations marked NASB are taken from the *New American
Standard Bible,* © Copyright 1960, 1995 by The Lockman Foundation. Used by permission;
and NIV are taken from the *Holy Bible, New International Version*®. *NIV*®. Copyright ©
1973, 1978, 1984 International Bible Society. Used by permission of Zondervan. All
rights reserved. The author has added italics to Scripture quotations for emphasis.

LCCN 2009934572
ISBN 978-1-4347-6636-6
eISBN 978-1-4347-0096-4

© 1982 Warren W. Wiersbe

First edition of *Be Wise* published by Victor Books® in 1982 ©
Warren W. Wiersbe, ISBN 978-0-89693-304-0

The Team: Karen Lee-Thorp, Amy Kiechlin, Sarah Schultz, Jack Campbell, and Karen Athen
Series Cover Design: John Hamilton Design
Cover Photo: Veer Inc.

Printed in the United States of America
Second Edition 2010

5 6 7 8 9 10

092613

To

Maynard and Ruth Mathewson

choice servants of the Lord who have (like the household of Stephanas) "devoted themselves to the ministry of the saints"

CONTENTS

THE BIG IDEA

An Introduction to *Be Wise*
by Ken Baugh

Have you ever questioned Jesus' wisdom in choosing the twelve disciples? Not long ago, I found an interesting evaluation from a fictitious management consulting firm on the Internet advising Jesus against choosing eleven of His twelve candidates for disciples. The letter reads as follows:

To: Jesus, Son of Joseph, Woodcrafter Carpenter Shop, Nazareth
From: Jordan Management Consultants, Jerusalem

Dear Sir:

Thank you for submitting the resumes of the twelve men you have picked for management positions in your new organization. All of them have now taken our battery of tests; we have not only run the results through our computer, but also arranged personal interviews for each of them with our psychologist and vocational aptitude consultant.

It is the staff's opinion that most of your nominees are lacking in the background, education and vocational aptitude for the type of enterprise you are undertaking. They do not have the team concept. We would recommend that you continue your search for persons of experience in managerial ability and proven capability.

Simon Peter is emotionally unstable and given to fits of temper. Andrew has no qualities of leadership. The two brothers, James and John, sons of Zebedee, place personal interests above company loyalty. Thomas demonstrates a questioning attitude that would tend to undermine morale.

We feel it is our duty to tell you that Matthew has been blacklisted by the Greater Jerusalem Better Business Bureau. James, the son of Alphaeus, and Thaddaeus definitely have radical leanings, and they both registered a high score on the manic depressive scale.

One of the candidates, however, shows great potential. He is a man of ability and resourcefulness, meets people well, has a keen business mind and has contacts in high places. He is highly motivated, ambitious and responsible. We recommend Judas Iscariot as your controller and right-hand man. All of the other profiles are self-explanatory.

We wish you every success in your new venture.

Sincerely yours,

Jordan Management Consultants

(Courtesy of Servant Quarters, www.servant.org/pa_m.htm)

Even though this is a humorous account, it drives home the radical difference between human and divine wisdom. Jesus drew from a different source of wisdom in choosing His disciples than this fictitious management consulting firm. They drew their criteria for the best candidate from the ways of the world, but Jesus drew His criteria from the ways of the Word. The ways of the world are drawn from finite human perspectives that are limited to human experience and tainted by sin. The ways of the Word are drawn from the perfect character and nature of the infinite God. Therefore, a wise person, when faced with a problem he cannot figure out, will seek the advice of the Word rather than the world. This is how the apostle Paul advised those who belonged to the church in Corinth to deal with the rampant problems within their church.

As you read through 1 Corinthians, you will quickly discover that this church had a daunting list of problems that were undermining the effectiveness of their witness and the vitality of their faith. Some church members were grumbling against Paul and his nonintellectual approach to evangelism (chapters 1—4). Some were living in unbelievable sexual sin (chapter 5), while others were suing each other in court (chapter 6). Members had questions about whether or not to get married or stay single, questions about divorce (chapter 7), questions about eating meat sacrificed to idols (chapters 8–10), and questions about how women should dress during worship (chapter 11). The rich were insulting the less affluent at the Lord's Supper (chapter 11), the use of spiritual gifts was tainted with pride (chapters 12—14), and some people were skeptical about the future resurrection of the dead (chapter 15).

The apostle Paul was so concerned about the people in this church that he wrote one of the most practical of all his letters, advising the Corinthians to apply spiritual wisdom to their worldly problems. In fact, I believe you could sum up 1 Corinthians like this: God's wisdom applied to worldly problems produces supernatural results.

You and I will always be faced with problems. Some problems we bring on ourselves, while others come as a normal part of life. The question is, where will you go to find the answers? Will you go to the world or the Word? I believe if you go to God's wisdom found in the pages of His Word, you will discover divine solutions to your problems.

But here's the million-dollar question: How can I know I can trust that the Bible is a perfect record of God's wisdom? How can I know that the Bible isn't just some book written by men? Well, let's go to the Bible to see if we can find the answer.

The Bible clearly affirms its divine authorship. "All Scripture is God-breathed and is useful for teaching, rebuking, correcting and training in righteousness, so that the man of God may be thoroughly equipped for every good work" (2 Tim. 3:16–17 NIV). "All Scripture" includes both Old and New Testaments as God-inspired. The apostle Peter affirms divine inspiration of the Bible as well: "Above all, you must understand that no prophecy of Scripture came about by the prophet's own interpretation. For prophecy never had its origin in the will of man, but men spoke from God as they were carried along by the Holy Spirit" (2 Peter 1:20–21 NIV). And the writer of Hebrews declares: "For the word of God is living and active" (Heb. 4:12 NIV).

The Bible is a divinely inspired collection of sixty-six books, each containing the perfect wisdom of God. And I encourage you, as you study 1 Corinthians, to focus on issues going on in your life and notice how Paul draws from God's Word to provide divine solutions to the Corinthians' problems. I believe that if you apply God's wisdom to your problems, you will experience supernatural results.

***

Dr. Wiersbe's commentaries have been a source of guidance and strength to me over the many years that I have been a pastor. His unique style is not overly academic, but theologically sound. He explains the deep truths of Scripture in a way that everyone can understand and apply. Whether you're a Bible scholar or a brand-new believer in Christ, you will benefit, as I have, from Warren's insights. With your Bible in one hand and Dr. Wiersbe's commentary in the other, you will be able to accurately unpack the deep truths of God's Word and learn how to apply them to your life.

Drink deeply, my friend, of the truths of God's Word, for in them you will find Jesus Christ, and there is freedom, peace, assurance, and joy.

—Ken Baugh
Pastor of Coast Hills Community Church
Aliso Viejo, California

A WORD FROM THE AUTHOR

The Christians in Corinth prided themselves in their spiritual gifts and knowledge. Yet something was radically wrong with their personal lives and with their local assembly.

Paul had what they needed—true spiritual wisdom. Not the wisdom of the world, but the wisdom that comes only from God.

We need this same wisdom today, and this letter is a good place to start discovering it. Paul tells us how to be wise about the message and the ministry of the gospel, so that we will not get trapped into "fan clubs" for religious leaders. He tells us what kind of order we should have in our worship and how we should discover and develop our spiritual gifts. He also tells us how to keep our lives clean so that we glorify God and escape the pollutions of the world.

In this brief expository study, we obviously cannot deal with all the challenging details of a large epistle like 1 Corinthians. It is my aim to explain the main lessons of the letter and to make them practical for our lives and our local churches. May the Lord assist us in receiving His spiritual wisdom and applying it personally.

—Warren W. Wiersbe

BACKGROUND OF THE CHURCH AT CORINTH

Paul came to Corinth about the fall of AD 50 and founded the church, remaining there eighteen months (Acts 18:1–17). He then went to Ephesus (vv. 18–19).

Word that there were problems in the church led him to write a letter, which we do not have (1 Cor. 5:9). This "lost letter" must not have accomplished what he desired, because further word came to Paul from "the house of Chloe" that there were serious problems in the Corinthian congregation (1 Cor. 7:1; 16:17–18).

In response to this letter and the bad news he received, Paul wrote the letter we know as 1 Corinthians. He wrote it from Ephesus about AD 57.

There was a faction in the church that refused to acknowledge Paul's apostolic authority. So the apostle made a "hasty visit" to Corinth, but the results were very unsatisfactory (2 Cor. 2:1; 12:14; 13:1). He then wrote them a "sharp letter" (2 Cor. 7:8–12), which was carried by Titus.

Paul met Titus at Troas (2 Cor. 2:12–13; 7:6–16) and received the good news that the church had obeyed Paul's orders and disciplined the leader of the opposition. Paul then wrote 2 Corinthians.

A SUGGESTED OUTLINE OF THE BOOK OF 1 CORINTHIANS

Theme: God's wisdom
Key verses: 1 Corinthians 2:6–8

I. Greeting (1 Corinthians 1:1–3)
II. Reproof: The Report of Sin in the Church
   (1 Corinthians 1:4—6:20)
   A. Divisions in the church (1 Corinthians 1:4—4:21)
   B. Discipline in the church (1 Corinthians 5)
   C. Disputes in the courts (1 Corinthians 6:1–8)
   D. Defilement in the world (1 Corinthians 6:9–20)
III. Instruction: The Reply to Their Questions
   (1 Corinthians 7:1—16:12)
   A. Marriage (1 Corinthians 7)
   B. Food offered to idols (1 Corinthians 8—10)
   C. Church ordinances (1 Corinthians 11)
   D. Spiritual gifts (1 Corinthians 12:1—14:40)
   E. The resurrection (1 Corinthians 15)
   F. The offering (1 Corinthians 16:1–12)
IV. Conclusion (1 Corinthians 16:13–24)

Chapter One

BE WISE ABOUT THE CHRISTIAN'S CALLING

(1 Corinthians 1)

J esus, yes! The church, no!" Remember when that slogan was popular among young people in the '60s? They certainly could have used it with sincerity in Corinth back in AD 56, because the local church there was in serious trouble. Sad to say, the problems did not stay within the church family; they were known by the unbelievers outside the church.

To begin with, the church at Corinth was a *defiled* church. Some of its members were guilty of sexual immorality; others got drunk; still others were using the grace of God to excuse worldly living. It was also a *divided* church, with at least four different groups competing for leadership (1 Cor. 1:12). This meant it was a *disgraced* church. Instead of glorifying God, it was hindering the progress of the gospel.

How did this happen? The members of the church permitted the sins of the city to get into the local assembly. Corinth was a polluted city, filled with every kind of vice and worldly pleasure. About the lowest accusation you could make against a man in that day would be to call him a "Corinthian." People would know what you were talking about.

Corinth was also a proud, philosophical city, with many itinerant teachers promoting their speculations. Unfortunately, this philosophical approach was applied to the gospel by some members of the church, and this fostered division. The congregation was made up of different "schools of thought" instead of being united behind the gospel message.

If you want to know what Corinth was like, read Romans 1:18–32. Paul wrote the Roman epistle while in Corinth, and he could have looked out the window and seen the very sins that he listed!

Of course, when you have proud people depending on human wisdom, adopting the lifestyle of the world, you are going to have problems. In order to help them solve their problems, Paul opened his letter by reminding them of their *calling in Christ.* He pointed out three important aspects of this calling.

1. CALLED TO BE HOLY (1:1–9)

Paul first attacked the serious problem of defilement in the church, yet he said nothing about the problem itself. Instead, he took the positive approach and reminded the believers of their high and holy position in Jesus Christ. In 1 Corinthians 1:1–9, he described the church that God sees; in 1 Corinthians 1:10–31, he described the church that men see. What we are in Jesus Christ *positionally* ought to be what we practice in daily life, but often we fail.

Note the characteristics of the church because of our holy calling in Jesus Christ.

Set apart by God (vv. 1–3). The word *church* in the Greek language means "a called-out people." Each church has two addresses: a geographic address ("at Corinth") and a spiritual address ("in Christ Jesus"). The church is made up of saints, that is, people who have been "sanctified" or "set apart" by God. A saint is not a dead person who has been honored by men because of his or her holy life. No, Paul wrote to *living* saints, people who, through faith in Jesus Christ, had been set apart for God's special enjoyment and use.

In other words, every true believer is a saint because every true believer has been set apart by God and for God.

A Christian photographer friend told me about a lovely wedding that he "covered." The bride and groom came out of the church, heading for the limousine, when the bride suddenly left her husband and ran to a car parked across the street! The motor was running and a man was at the wheel, and off they drove, leaving the bridegroom speechless. The driver of the "getaway car" turned out to be an old boyfriend of the bride, a man who had boasted that "he could get her any time he wanted her." Needless to say, the husband had the marriage annulled.

When a man and woman pledge their love to each other, they are set apart for each other; and any other relationship outside of marriage is sinful. Just so, the Christian belongs completely to Jesus Christ; he is set apart for Him and Him alone. But he is also a part of a worldwide fellowship, the church, "all that in every place call upon the name of Jesus Christ" (1 Cor. 1:2). A defiled and unfaithful believer not only sins against the Lord, but he also sins against his fellow Christians.

Enriched by God's grace (vv. 4–6). Salvation is a gracious gift from God; but when you are saved, you are also given spiritual gifts. (Paul explained this in detail in 1 Cor. 12—14.) The Greek word translated "enriched" gives us our English word *plutocrat,* "a very wealthy person." The Corinthians were especially rich in spiritual gifts (2 Cor. 8:7) but were not using these gifts in a spiritual manner. The fact that God has called us, set us apart, and enriched us ought to encourage us to live holy lives.

Expecting Jesus to return (v. 7). Paul will have a great deal to say about this truth in 1 Corinthians 15. Christians who are looking for their Savior will want to keep their lives above reproach (1 John 2:28—3:3).

Depending on God's faithfulness (vv. 8–9). The work of God was confirmed *in* them (1 Cor. 1:6), but it was also confirmed *to* them in the Word. This is a legal term that refers to the guarantee that settles a transaction. We have the witness of the Spirit within us and the witness of the Word before us, guaranteeing that God will keep His "contract" with us and save us to the very end. This guarantee is certainly not an excuse for sin! Rather, it is the basis for a growing relationship of love, trust, and obedience.

Now, in the light of these great truths, how could the people in the Corinthian assembly get involved in the sins of the world and the flesh? They were an elect people, an enriched people, and an established people. They were saints, set apart for the glory of God! Alas, their practice was not in accord with their position.

When Paul mentioned the word *fellowship* in 1 Corinthians 1:9, he introduced a second aspect of the Christian's calling.

2. CALLED INTO FELLOWSHIP (1:10–25)

Having mentioned the problem of defilement in the church, now Paul turned to the matter of division in the church. Division has always been a problem among God's people, and almost every New Testament epistle deals with this topic or mentions it in one way or another. Even the twelve apostles did not always get along with each other.

In 1 Corinthians 1:13, Paul asked his readers three important questions, and these three questions are the key to this long paragraph.

(1) Is Christ divided (vv. 10–13a)? The verb means, "Has Christ been divided and different parts handed out to different people?" The very idea is grotesque and must be rejected. Paul did not preach one Christ, Apollos another, and Peter another. There is but one Savior and one gospel (Gal. 1:6–9). How, then, did the Corinthians create this four-way division? Why were there quarrels ("contentions") among them?

One answer is that they were looking at the gospel from a philosophical point of view. Corinth was a city filled with teachers and philosophers, all of whom wanted to share their "wisdom."

Another answer is that human nature enjoys following human leaders. We tend to identify more with spiritual leaders who help us and whose ministry we understand and enjoy. Instead of emphasizing the *message* of the Word, the Corinthians emphasized the *messenger*. They got their eyes off the Lord and on the Lord's servants, and this led to competition.

Paul will point out in 1 Corinthians 3 that there can be no competition among true servants of God. It is sinful for church members to compare pastors, or for believers to follow human leaders as disciples of men and not disciples of Jesus Christ. The "personality cults" in the church today are in direct disobedience to the Word of God. Only Jesus Christ should have the place of preeminence (Col. 1:18).

Paul used several key words in this section to emphasize the unity of the saints in Christ. He called his readers *brethren,* reminding them that they belonged to one family. The phrase "perfectly joined together" is a medical term that describes the unity of the human body *knit together.* So, they had a *loving* union as members of the body. They were also identified by the name of Jesus Christ. This was probably a reference to their baptism.

We do not know who the people were who belonged to "the house of Chloe," but we commend them for their courage and devotion. They did not try to hide the problems. They were burdened about them; they went to the right person with them; and they were not afraid to be mentioned by Paul. This was not the kind of "cloak and dagger" affair that we often see in churches—activities that usually make the problem worse and not better.

Paul was the minister who founded the church, so most of the members would have been converted through his ministry. Apollos followed Paul (Acts 18:24–28) and had an effective ministry. We have no record that Peter (Cephas) ever visited Corinth, unless 1 Corinthians 9:5 records it. Each of these men had a different personality and a different approach to the ministry of the Word; *yet they were one* (1 Cor. 3:3–8; 4:6).

(2) Were you baptized in the name of Paul (vv. 13b–17)? Keep in mind that baptism was an important matter in the New Testament church. When a sinner trusted Christ and was baptized, he cut himself off from his old life and often was rejected by his family and friends. It cost something to be baptized in that day.

Just as Jesus did not baptize people (John 4:1–2), so both Peter (Acts 10:48) and Paul allowed their associates to baptize the new converts. Until the church grew in Corinth, Paul did some of the baptizing; but that was not his main ministry. In this section, Paul was not minimizing baptism, but rather was putting it into its proper perspective, because the Corinthians were making too much of it. "I was baptized by Apollos!" one would boast, while another would say, "Oh, but I was baptized by Paul!"

It is wrong to identify any man's name with your baptism other than the name of Jesus Christ. To do so is to create division. I have read accounts about people who had to be baptized by a certain preacher, using special water (usually from the Jordan River), on a special day, as though these are the matters that are important! Instead of honoring the Lord Jesus Christ and promoting the unity of the church, these people exalt men and create disunity.

Crispus had been the ruler of the synagogue in Corinth (Acts 18:8); and Gaius was probably the man Paul lived with when he wrote Romans (Rom. 16:23). "The household of Stephanas" (1 Cor. 1:16) is probably described in part in 1 Corinthians 16:15–18. Apparently Paul did not carry with him a record of the names of all the people he baptized. It was sufficient that they were written in God's book.

(3) Was Paul crucified for you (vv. 18–25)? The mention of the cross in 1 Corinthians 1:17 introduced this long section on the power of the gospel versus the weakness of man's wisdom. It is interesting to see how Paul approached this problem of division in the church. First, he pointed to the unity of Christ: There is one Savior and one body. Then he reminded them of their baptism, a picture of their spiritual baptism into Christ's body (1 Cor. 12:13). Then he took them to the cross.

Crucifixion was not only a horrible death; it was a shameful death. It was illegal to crucify a Roman citizen. Crucifixion was never mentioned in polite society, any more than we today would discuss over dinner the gas chamber or the electric chair.

The key word in this paragraph is *wisdom;* it is used eight times. The key idea that Paul expressed is that we dare not mix man's wisdom with God's revealed message. The entire section on wisdom (1 Cor. 1:17—2:16) presents a number of contrasts between the revealed Word of God and the wisdom of men.

God's wisdom is revealed primarily in the cross of Jesus Christ, but not everybody sees this. Paul pointed out that there are three different attitudes toward the cross.

Some stumble at the cross (v. 23a). This was the attitude of the Jews, because their emphasis was on miraculous signs and the cross appears to be weakness. Jewish history is filled with miraculous events, from the exodus out of Egypt to the days of Elijah and Elisha. When Jesus was ministering on earth, the Jewish leaders repeatedly asked Him to perform a sign from heaven; but He refused.

The Jewish nation did not understand their own sacred Scriptures. They looked for a Messiah who would come like a mighty conqueror and defeat all their enemies. He would then set up His kingdom and return the glory to Israel. The question of the apostles in Acts 1:6 shows how strong this hope was among the Jews.

At the same time, their scribes noticed in the Old Testament that the Messiah would suffer and die. Passages like Psalm 22 and Isaiah 53 pointed toward a different kind of Messiah, and the scholars could not reconcile these two seemingly contradictory prophetic images. They did not understand that their Messiah had to suffer and die before He could enter into

His glory (Luke 24:13–35), and that the future messianic kingdom was to be preceded by the age of the church.

Because the Jews were looking for power and great glory, they stumbled at the weakness of the cross. How could anybody put faith in an unemployed carpenter from Nazareth who died the shameful death of a common criminal? But the gospel of Jesus Christ is "the power of God unto salvation" (Rom. 1:16). Rather than a testimony of weakness, the cross is a tremendous instrument of power! After all, the "weakness of God [in the cross] is stronger than men" (1 Cor. 1:25).

Some laugh at the cross (v. 23b). This was the response of the Greeks. To them, the cross was foolishness. The Greeks emphasized wisdom; we still study the profound writings of the Greek philosophers. But they saw no wisdom in the cross, for they looked at the cross from a human point of view. Had they seen it from God's viewpoint, they would have discerned the wisdom of God's great plan of salvation.

Paul called on three men to bear witness: the wise (the expert), the scribe (the interpreter and writer), and the disputer (the philosopher and debater). He asked them one question: Through your studies into man's wisdom, have you come to know God in a personal way? They all must answer no! The fact that they laugh at the cross and consider it foolishness is evidence that they are perishing.

Paul quoted Isaiah 29:14 in 1 Corinthians 1:19, proving that God has written a big "0—Failure!" over the wisdom of men. In his address on Mars Hill, Paul dared to tell the philosophers that Greek and Roman history were but "times of this ignorance" (Acts 17:30). He was not suggesting that they knew nothing, because Paul knew too well that the Greek thinkers had made some achievements. However, their wisdom did not enable them to find God and experience salvation.

Some believe and experience the power and the wisdom of the cross (v. 24). Paul did not alter his message when he turned from a Jewish audience to a Greek one: He preached Christ crucified. "The foolishness of preaching" (1 Cor. 1:21) does not mean that the *act* of preaching is foolish, but rather the content of the message. The New International Version states it, "Through the foolishness of what was preached," and this is correct.

Those who have been called by God's grace, and who have responded by faith (2 Thess. 2:13–14), realize that Christ is God's power and God's wisdom. Not the Christ of the manger, or the temple, or the marketplace—but the Christ of the cross. It is in the death of Christ that God has revealed the foolishness of man's wisdom and the weakness of man's power.

We are called into fellowship because of our union with Jesus Christ: He died for us; we were baptized in His name; we are identified with His cross. What a wonderful basis for spiritual unity!

3. Called to Glorify God (1:26–31)

The Corinthians had a tendency to be "puffed up" with pride (1 Cor. 4:6, 18–19; 5:2). But the gospel of God's grace leaves no room for personal boasting. God is not impressed with our looks, our social position, our achievements, our natural heritage, or our financial status. Note that Paul wrote *many,* not *any.* In the New Testament, we do meet some believers with "high social standing," but there are not many of them. The description Paul gave of the converts was certainly not a flattering one (1 Cor. 6:9–11).

Paul reminded them of what they were (v. 26). They were not wise, mighty, or noble. God called them, not *because of* what they were, but *in spite of* what they were! The Corinthian church was composed primarily of ordinary people who were terrible sinners. Before his conversion, Paul had been very self-righteous; he had to give up his religion in order to go to heaven! The Corinthians were at the other end of the spectrum, and yet they were not too sinful for God to reach and save them.

Paul reminded the Corinthians of why God called them (vv. 27–29). God chose the foolish, the weak, the base ("low born"), and the despised to show the proud world their need and His grace. The lost world admires birth, social status, financial success, power, and recognition. But none of these things can guarantee eternal life.

The message and miracle of God's grace in Jesus Christ utterly confounds ("puts to shame") the high and mighty people of this world. The wise of this world cannot understand how God changes sinners into saints, and the mighty of this world are helpless to duplicate the miracle. God's "foolishness" confounds the wise; God's "weakness" confounds the mighty!

The annals of church history are filled with the accounts of great sinners whose lives were transformed by the power of the gospel. In my own ministry, as in the ministry of most pastors and preachers, I have seen amazing things take place that the lawyers and psychologists could not understand. We have seen delinquent teenagers become successful students and useful citizens. We have seen marriages restored and homes reclaimed, much to the amazement of the courts.

And why does God reveal the foolishness and the weakness of this present world system, even with its philosophy and religion? "That no flesh should glory in his presence" (1 Cor. 1:29). Salvation must be wholly of grace; otherwise, God cannot get the glory.

It is this truth that Paul wanted to get across to the Corinthians, because they were guilty of glorying in men (1 Cor. 3:21). If we glory in men—even godly men like Peter and Paul and Apollos—we are robbing God of the glory that He alone deserves. It was this sinful attitude of pride that was helping to cause division in the church.

Finally, Paul reminded the Corinthians of all they had in Jesus Christ (vv. 30–31). Since every believer is "in Christ," and he has all that he needs, why compete with each other or compare yourselves with each other? It is the Lord who has done it all! "He that glorieth, let him glory in the Lord" (1 Cor. 1:31, a quotation from Jer. 9:24, quoted again in 2 Cor. 10:17).

The spiritual blessings that we need are not abstractions that elude our grasp; they are all in a person, Jesus Christ. He is our wisdom (Col. 2:3), our righteousness (2 Cor. 5:21), our sanctification (John 17:19), and our redemption (Rom. 3:24).

Actually, the emphasis here is that God shows His wisdom by means of the righteousness, sanctification, and redemption that we have in Christ. Each of these theological words carries a special meaning for Christians. *Righteousness* has to do with our standing before God. We are justified: God declares us righteous in Jesus Christ. But we are also *sanctified,* set apart to belong to God and to serve Him. *Redemption* emphasizes the fact that we are set free because Jesus Christ paid the price for us on the cross. This will lead to complete redemption when Christ returns.

So, in one sense, we have the three tenses of salvation given here: We *have been saved* from the penalty of sin (righteousness); we *are being saved* from the power of sin (sanctification); and we *shall be saved* from the presence of sin (redemption). And every believer has all of these blessings in Jesus Christ!

Therefore, why glory in men? What does Paul have that you do not have? Does Peter have more of Jesus Christ than you do? (It was likely that Jesus Christ had more of Peter, but that is another matter!) We should glory in the Lord and not in ourselves or our spiritual leaders.

As you review this chapter, you can see the mistakes that the Corinthians were making, mistakes that helped to create problems in their church. They were not living up to their holy calling, but were instead following the standards of the world. They ignored the fact that they were called into a wonderful spiritual fellowship with the Lord and with each other. Instead, they were identifying with human leaders and creating divisions in the church. Instead of glorifying God and His grace, they were pleasing themselves and boasting about men.

They were a defiled church, a divided church, a disgraced church!

But, before we pass judgment on them, we should examine our own churches and our own lives. We have been called to be holy, called into fellowship, and called to glorify God.

Are we living up to this calling?

QUESTIONS FOR PERSONAL REFLECTION
OR GROUP DISCUSSION

1. Have you ever experienced conflict in a church you've belonged to? If so, how did it affect you?

2. What do you think it means to be "called to be holy" (1:2 NIV)? How should this work against divisions in the church?

3. Why do you suppose divisions have always been a problem among God's people?

4. What arguments does Paul use in 1 Corinthians 1 for eliminating such divisions?

5. When the message of the cross is presented, why do some people stumble at it? Why do some laugh?

6. What did Paul say to counteract the Corinthians' tendency toward pride?

7. What kind of people did the church at Corinth consist of?

8. Why did God choose such an unlikely bunch?

9. Why did Paul emphasize to the Corinthians that salvation is wholly of grace?

10. What do you learn from 1 Corinthians 1 that could help you deal with conflict in the church?

Chapter Two

BE WISE ABOUT THE CHRISTIAN MESSAGE

(1 Corinthians 2)

My wife was at the wheel of our car as we drove to Chicago, and I was in the copilot's seat reading the page proofs of another author's book that a publisher had asked me to review. Occasionally I would utter a grunt, and then a groan, and finally I shook my head and said, "Oh, no! I can't believe it!"

"I take it you don't like the book," she said. "Something wrong with it?"

"You bet there is!" I replied. "Just about everything is wrong with it, because this man does not know what the message of the gospel really is!"

There was a time, however, when that author had been faithful to the gospel. But over the years, he had begun to take a philosophical (and, I fear, political) approach to the gospel. The result was a hybrid message that was no gospel at all.

It is worth noting that when Paul ministered in Corinth, he obeyed our Lord's commission and preached the gospel. There is a beautiful parallel between Matthew 28:18–20 and Acts 18:1–11.

Christ's Commission (Matt. 28:18–20)	Paul's Ministry (Acts 18:1–11)
"Go ye therefore" (v. 19)	Paul came to Corinth (v. 1)
"teach all nations" (v. 19)	many heard and believed (v. 8)
"baptizing them" (v. 19)	and were baptized (v. 8)
"teaching them" (v. 20)	for a year and six months he taught the Word (v. 11)
"Lo, I am with you" (v. 20)	"For I am with thee" (v. 10)

What had happened at Corinth is happening in churches today: Men are mixing philosophy (man's wisdom) with God's revealed message, and this is causing confusion and division. Different preachers have their own "interpretation" to God's message, and some even invent their own vocabulary!

Paul explained the three fundamentals of the gospel message and urged his readers to return to these fundamentals.

1. The Gospel Centers in the Death of Christ (2:1–5)

Paul reminded the Corinthians of his approach (vv. 1–2). The opening words, "And I," can be translated "Accordingly," on the basis of 1 Corinthians 1:31—the glory of God. Paul had not come to Corinth to glorify himself or to start a religious "fan club." He had come to glorify God.

The itinerant philosophers and teachers depended on their wisdom and eloquence to gain followers. The city of Corinth was filled with such "spellbinders." Paul did not depend on eloquent speech or clever arguments; he simply declared God's Word in the power of the Spirit. He was an ambassador, not a "Christian salesman."

Had he used spectacular speech and philosophy, Paul would have exalted himself and hidden the very Christ he came to proclaim! God had sent him to preach the gospel "not with wisdom of words, lest the cross of Christ should be made of none effect" (1 Cor. 1:17).

A certain church had a beautiful stained-glass window just behind the pulpit. It depicted Jesus Christ on the cross. One Sunday there was a guest minister who was much smaller than the regular pastor. A little girl listened to the guest for a time, then turned to her mother and asked, "Where is the man who usually stands there so we can't see Jesus?"

Too many preachers of the Word so magnify themselves and their gifts that they fail to reveal the glory of Jesus Christ. Paul gloried in the cross of Christ (Gal. 6:14) and made it the center of his message.

Then Paul reminded the Corinthians of his attitude (vv. 3–4). Though he was an apostle, Paul came to them as a humble servant. He did not depend on himself; he became nothing that Christ might be everything. In later years, Paul brought this up again and contrasted himself to the false teachers who had invaded Corinth (2 Cor. 10:1–12). Paul had learned that when he was weak, God made him strong.

Paul depended on the power of the Holy Spirit. It was not his experience or ability that gave his ministry its power; it was the work of the Spirit of God. His preaching was a "demonstration," not a "performance." The word translated "demonstration" means "legal proof presented in court." The Holy Spirit used Paul's preaching to change lives, and that was all the proof Paul needed that his message was from God. Wicked sinners were transformed by the power of God (1 Cor. 6:9–11)!

However, we must note that Paul is not telling ministers deliberately to preach poorly, or to avoid using the gifts God gave them. Men like Charles Spurgeon and George Whitefield were gifted orators whose words carried power, *but they did not depend on their natural talents.* They trusted the Spirit of God to work in the hearts of their hearers, and He did. Those who minister the Word must prepare and use every gift God has given them—but they must not put their confidence in themselves (2 Cor. 3:5).

Finally, Paul reminded them of his aim (v. 5). He wanted them to trust in God and not in the messenger God sent. Had he depended on human wisdom and presented the plan of salvation as a philosophical system, then the Corinthians would have put their trust in an *explanation*. Because Paul declared the Word of God in the power of God, his converts put their faith in a *demonstration:* They experienced God at work in their own lives.

Years ago, a wise Christian said to me, "When you are leading people to Christ, never tell them that they are saved because they have done this or that. It is the job of the Holy Spirit to witness to people that they are saved. Unless He is at work, there can be no salvation." Wise counsel, indeed!

I recall a fine professional man who faithfully attended a church I pastored—a man who was unsaved, but not antagonistic to the gospel. Many of us prayed for him as he continued to listen to the Word. One day a Christian friend of his decided to win him to Christ, or else! He spent several hours presenting argument after argument, and finally the man "prayed the sinner's prayer." Then he stopped attending church! Why? Because he had been talked into something that was not real, and he knew he could not follow through. Later on, he *did* trust Christ and, through the Spirit, have the assurance of salvation. Up to that point, if anybody asked him if he were saved, he would reply, "Sure—Tom told me I was saved!" What a difference when the Spirit gives the assurance!

The gospel is still God's power to change men's lives (Rom. 1:16). Effectiveness in evangelism does not depend on our arguments or persuasive gimmicks but on the power of the Spirit of God at work in our lives and through the Word that we share.

2. THE GOSPEL IS PART OF THE FATHER'S ETERNAL PLAN (2:6–9)

Salvation was purchased by the Son, but it was planned by the Father. Those who talk about "the simple gospel" are both right and wrong. Yes, the message of the gospel is simple enough for an illiterate pagan to understand, believe, and be saved. But it is also so profound that the most brilliant theologian cannot fathom its depths.

There is a "wisdom of God" in the gospel that challenges the keenest intellect. However, this wisdom is not for the masses of lost sinners, nor is it for the immature believers. It is for the mature believers who are growing in their understanding of the Word of God. (The word *perfect* in 1 Corinthians 2:6 means "mature." See 1 Cor. 3:1–4.) Perhaps here Paul was answering those in the church who were promoting Apollos, who was an eloquent and profound preacher (Acts 18:24–28).

Let's notice the characteristics of this wisdom.

This wisdom comes from God, not man (v. 7). This wisdom tells the mature saint about the vast eternal plan that God has for His people and His creation. The wisest of the "princes of this world [age]" could not invent or discover this marvelous wisdom that Paul shared from God.

This wisdom has been hidden (v. 7). That is why it is called a mystery, for in the New Testament, a mystery is a "sacred secret," a truth hidden in past ages but now revealed to the people of God. It was Paul whom God used in a special way to share the various "mysteries" that are related to the gospel (Eph. 3); but note the repetition of the pronoun "we." Paul did not leave out the other apostles.

This wisdom involves God's ordination (v. 7). This means that God made the plan, set it in motion, and will see to it that it will succeed. The great plan of redemption was not a hasty afterthought on the part of God after He saw what man had done. Though all of this boggles our minds, we must accept the Bible truth of divine election and predestination. Even the death of Jesus Christ was ordained of God (Acts 2:22–23; 1 Peter 1:18–20), though men were held responsible for the wicked deed. One of the secrets of an effective prayer life is to lay hold of God's purposes by faith (Acts 4:23–31).

This wisdom results in the glory of God's people (v. 7). One of the greatest expositions of this "plan of the ages" is in Ephesians 1. Three times in that passage, Paul explained that all of this is done for God's glory (Eph. 1:6, 12, 14). It is a staggering thought that we shall one day share in the very glory of God (John 17:22–24; Rom. 8:28–30)!

This wisdom is hidden from the unsaved world (v. 8). Who are "the princes of this world [age]" that Paul mentions? Certainly the men who were in charge of government when Jesus was on earth did not know who He was (Acts 3:17; 4:25–28). When Jesus on the cross prayed, "Father, forgive them; for they know not what they do" (Luke 23:34), He was echoing this truth. Their ignorance did not *excuse* their sin, of course, because every evidence had been given by the Lord and they should have believed.

But there is another possibility. Paul may have been referring to the *spiritual and demonic rulers of this present age* (Rom. 8:38; Col. 2:15; Eph. 6:12ff.). This would make more sense in 1 Corinthians 2:6, for certainly Pilate, Herod, and the other rulers were not recognized for any special wisdom. The wisdom of this age has its origin in the rulers of this age, of which Satan is the prince (John 12:31; 14:30; 16:11). Of course, the spiritual rulers would have to work in and through the human rulers. So perhaps we must not press the distinction (John 13:2, 27).

But if this interpretation is true, then it opens up a challenging area of consideration. The satanic forces, including Satan himself, did not understand God's great eternal plan! They could understand from the Old Testament Scriptures that the Son of God would be born and die, but they could not grasp the full significance of the cross because these truths were hidden by God. In fact, it is now, through the church, that these truths are being revealed to the principalities and powers (Eph. 3:10).

Satan thought that Calvary was God's great defeat; but it turned out to be God's greatest victory and *Satan's defeat* (Col. 2:15)! From the time of our Lord's birth into this world, Satan had tried to kill Him, because Satan did not fully understand the vast results of Christ's death and resurrection.

Had the demonic rulers known, they would not have "engineered" the death of Christ. (Of course, all of this was part of God's eternal plan. It was God who was in control, not Satan.)

Finally, this wisdom applies to the believer's life today (v. 9). This verse is often used at funerals and applied to heaven, but the basic application is to the Christian's life *today*. The next verse makes it clear that God is revealing these things to us here and now.

This verse is a quotation (with adaptation) from Isaiah 64:4. The immediate context relates it to Israel in captivity, awaiting God's deliverance. The nation had sinned and had been sent to Babylon for chastening. They cried out to God that He would come down to deliver them, and He did answer their prayer after seventy years of their exile. God had plans for His people, and they did not have to be afraid (Jer. 29:11).

Paul applied this principle to the church. Our future is secure in Jesus Christ no matter what our circumstances may be. In fact, God's plans for His own are so wonderful that our minds cannot begin to conceive of them or comprehend them! God has ordained this for our glory (1 Cor. 2:7). It is glory all the way from earth to heaven!

For those who love God, every day is a good day (Rom. 8:28). It may not *look* like a good day, or *feel* like it; but when God is working His plan, we can be sure of the best. It is when we fail to trust Him or obey Him, when our love for Him grows cold, that life takes on a somber hue. If we walk in God's wisdom, we will enjoy His blessings.

We have considered two fundamental truths of the gospel: This message centers in the death of Christ, and it is part of the Father's vast eternal plan. The believers at Corinth had forgotten the cost of their salvation; they had gotten their eyes off of the cross. They were also involved in minor matters—"baby toys"—because they had lost the wonder of the greatness of God's plan for them. They needed to return to the ministry of the Holy Spirit, and this would be Paul's next point.

3. THE GOSPEL IS REVEALED BY THE SPIRIT THROUGH THE WORD (2:10–16)

Our salvation involves all three persons in the Godhead (Eph. 1:3–14; 1 Peter 1:2). You cannot be saved apart from the Father's electing grace, the Son's loving sacrifice, and the Spirit's ministry of conviction and regeneration. It is not enough to say, "I believe in God." What God? Unless it is "the God and Father of our Lord Jesus Christ" (Eph. 1:3), there can be no salvation.

This trinitarian aspect of our salvation helps us to understand better some of the mysteries of our salvation. Many people get confused (or frightened) when they hear about election and predestination. As far as the Father is concerned, I was saved when He chose me in Christ before the foundation of the world (Eph. 1:4); but I knew nothing about that the night I was saved! It was a hidden part of God's wonderful eternal plan.

As far as God the Son is concerned, I was saved when He died for me on the cross. He died for the sins of the whole world, yet the whole world is not saved. This is where the Spirit comes in: As far as the Spirit is concerned, I was saved in May 1945 at a Youth for Christ rally where I heard Billy Graham (then a young evangelist) preach the gospel. It was then that the Holy Spirit applied the Word to my heart, I believed, and God saved me.

Paul pointed out four important ministries of the Holy Spirit of God.

(1) The Spirit indwells believers (v. 12). The very moment you trusted Jesus Christ, the Spirit of God entered your body and made it His temple (1 Cor. 6:19–20). He baptized you (identified you) into the body of Christ (1 Cor. 12:13). He sealed you (Eph. 1:13–14) and will remain with you (John 14:16). He is God's gift to you.

The Holy Spirit is the Spirit of liberty (2 Cor. 3:17). We have not received the "spirit of the world" because we have been called out of this world and no longer belong to it (John 17:14, 16). We are no longer under the authority of Satan and his world system.

Nor have we received a "spirit of bondage again to fear" (Rom. 8:15). The Holy Spirit ministers to us and makes the Father real to us. This ties in with 2 Timothy 1:7—"For God hath not given us the spirit of fear; but of power, and of love, and of a sound [disciplined] mind." We have a wealth of spiritual resources because the Spirit lives within us!

(2) The Spirit searches (vv. 10–11). I cannot know what is going on within your personality, but your human spirit within you knows. Neither can I know "the deep things of God" unless somehow I can enter into God's personality. I cannot do that—but by His Spirit, God has entered into my personality. Through the Holy Spirit, each believer becomes a sharer of the very life of God.

The Holy Spirit knows "the deep things of God" and reveals them to us. First Corinthians 2:10 makes it clear that "the deep things of God" is another description of "the things which God hath prepared for them that love him" (1 Cor. 2:9). God wants us to know *today* all the blessings of His grace that He has planned for us.

(3) The Spirit teaches (v. 13). Jesus promised that the Spirit would teach us (John 14:26) and guide us into truth (John 16:13). But we must note carefully the sequence here: The Spirit taught Paul from the Word, and Paul then taught the believers. The truth of God is found in the Word of God. And it is very important to note that these spiritual truths are given in specific *words*. In the Bible, we have much more than inspired thoughts; we have inspired *words*. "For I have given unto them the words which thou gavest me" (John 17:8).

Each of our four children has a different vocation. We have a pastor, a nurse, an electronics designer, and a secretary in a commercial real estate firm. Each of the children had to learn a specialized vocabulary in order to succeed. The only one I really understand is the pastor.

The successful Christian learns the vocabulary of the Spirit and makes use of it. He knows the meaning of justification, sanctification, adoption, propitiation, election, inspiration, and so forth. In understanding God's vocabulary, we come to understand God's Word and God's will for our lives. If the engineering student can grasp the technical terms of chemistry, physics, or electronics, why should it be difficult for Christians, taught by the Spirit, to grasp the vocabulary of Christian truth?

Yet I hear church members say, "Don't preach doctrine. Just give us heartwarming sermons that will encourage us!" Sermons based on what? If they are not based on doctrine, they will accomplish nothing! "But doctrine is so dull!" people complain. Not if it is presented the way the Bible presents it. Doctrine to me is exciting! What a thrill to be able to study the Bible and let the Spirit teach us "the deep things of God" (1 Cor. 2:10).

How does the Spirit teach the believer? He compares "spiritual things with spiritual." He reminds us of what He has taught us (John 14:26), relates that truth to something new, and then leads us into new truth and new applications of old truth. What a joy it is to sit before the pages of the Bible and let the Spirit reveal God's truth. The trouble is, many Christians are too busy for this kind of quiet meditation. What enrichment they are missing!

The Holy Spirit is like a householder who "bringeth forth out of his treasure things new and old" (Matt. 13:52). The new always comes out of the old and helps us better understand the old. God gives us new insights into old truths as we compare one part of Scripture with another. Jesus based His teaching on the Old Testament, yet people were amazed at what He taught because it was so fresh and exciting.

I suggest that you make time every day to read the Word and meditate on it. Follow a regular schedule in your reading, and give yourself time to pray, think, and meditate. Let the Spirit of God search the Word and teach you. The study and application of basic Bible doctrine can transform your life.

(4) The Spirit matures the believer (vv. 14–16). The contrast here is between the saved person (called "spiritual" because he is indwelt by the Spirit) and the unsaved person (called "natural" because he does not have the Spirit within). In 1 Corinthians 3:1–4, Paul will introduce a third kind of person, the "carnal man." He is the immature Christian, the one who lives on a childhood level because he will not feed on the Word and grow.

At one time, every Christian was "natural," having only the things of nature. When we trusted the Savior, the Spirit came in and we moved into the plane of "spiritual"—able to live in the realm of the Spirit. *Then we had to grow!* The unsaved man cannot receive the things of the Spirit because he does not believe in them and cannot understand them. But as the Christian day by day receives the things of the Spirit, he grows and matures.

One of the marks of maturity is discernment—the ability to penetrate beneath the surface of life and see things as they really are. Unsaved people "walk by sight" and really see nothing. They are spiritually blind. The maturing Christian grows in his spiritual discernment and develops the ability (with the Spirit's help) to understand more and more of the will and mind of God. The Corinthians lacked this discernment; they were spiritually ignorant.

To "have the mind of Christ" does not mean we are infallible and start playing God in the lives of other people. Nobody instructs God! (Paul quoted Isa. 40:13. Also see Rom. 11:33–36.) To "have the mind of Christ" means to look at life from the Savior's point of view, having His values and desires in mind. It means to think God's thoughts and not think as the world thinks.

The unsaved person does not understand the Christian; they live in two different worlds. But the Christian understands the unsaved person. First Corinthians 2:15 does not suggest that unsaved people cannot point out flaws in the believer's life (they often do), but that the unsaved man really cannot penetrate into the full understanding of what the Christian's life is all about. I like the New American Standard Bible's translation: "But he who is spiritual appraises all things, yet he himself is appraised by no one." That "no one" includes other Christians as well. We must be very careful not to become spiritual dictators in the lives of God's people (2 Cor. 1:24).

The Corinthian Christians were so wrapped up in the miraculous gifts of the Spirit that they were neglecting the basic ministries of the Spirit. And in their emphasis on the Spirit, they were also neglecting the Father and the Son.

Blessed are the balanced! And blessed are they who understand and share "all the counsel of God" (Acts 20:27).

QUESTIONS FOR PERSONAL REFLECTION
OR GROUP DISCUSSION

1. What goes through your mind when you have an opportunity to talk to an unbeliever about your faith?

2. What was Paul's unexpected strategy in sharing the gospel?

3. How did the Corinthians expect the gospel to be packaged?

4. How do people today expect the gospel to be packaged?

5. How does God's wisdom differ from the wisdom of men?

6. What is the "secret wisdom" Paul talked about? How is this wisdom revealed?

7. According to 2:12–16, what does the Holy Spirit do for us?

8. In practical terms, how does the Spirit teach the believer?

9. What do you think Paul meant when he said, "The spiritual man makes judgments about all things, but he himself is not subject to any man's judgment" (2:15 NIV)?

10. What does it mean that believers have the "mind of Christ"?

11. How can you cooperate with the Spirit's work?

Chapter Three

BE WISE ABOUT THE LOCAL CHURCH

(1 Corinthians 3)

B ritish Bible teacher Dr. G. Campbell Morgan had four sons; all
became ministers. Someone asked one of the grandsons if he
also would become a minister, and he replied, "No, I plan to
work for a living."

What is a pastor supposed to do? What really is "the work of the
ministry"? If we don't know, we will never know how to evaluate the
minister's work. Perhaps no issue creates more problems in the local
church than this one: How do we know when the pastor and church
leaders are really doing their job?

Paul painted three pictures of the church in this chapter and, using
these pictures, pointed out what the ministry is supposed to accomplish.
The church is a *family* and the goal is *maturity* (1 Cor. 3:1–4). The church
is a *field* and the goal is *quantity* (1 Cor. 3:5–9a). The church is a *temple*
and the goal is *quality* (1 Cor. 3:9b–23).

1. THE FAMILY—MATURITY (3:1–4)

Paul already explained that there are two kinds of people in the world—
natural (unsaved) and spiritual (saved). But now he explained that there

are two kinds of saved people: mature and immature (carnal). A Christian matures by allowing the Spirit to teach him and direct him by feeding on the Word. The immature Christian lives for the things of the flesh *(carnal* means "flesh") and has little interest in the things of the Spirit. Of course, some believers are immature because they have been saved only a short time, but that is not what Paul was discussing here.

Paul was the "spiritual father" who brought this family into being (1 Cor. 4:15). During the eighteen months he ministered in Corinth, Paul had tried to feed his spiritual children and help them mature in the faith. Just as in a human family, everybody helps the new baby grow and mature, so in the family of God we must encourage spiritual maturity.

What are the marks of maturity? For one thing, you can tell the mature person by his *diet*. As I write this chapter, we are watching our grandson and our granddaughter grow up. Becky is still being nursed by her mother, but Jonathan now sits at the table and uses his little cup and (with varying degrees of success) his tableware. As children grow, they learn to eat different food. They graduate (to use Paul's words) from milk to meat.

What is the difference? The usual answer is that "milk" represents the easy things in the Word, while "meat" represents the hard doctrines. But I disagree with that traditional explanation, and my proof is Hebrews 5:10–14. That passage seems to teach that "milk" represents what Jesus Christ did on earth, while "meat" concerns what He is doing now in heaven. The writer of Hebrews wanted to teach his readers about the present heavenly priesthood of Jesus Christ, but his readers were so immature, he could not do it (Heb. 6:1–4).

The Word of God is our spiritual food: milk (1 Peter 2:2), bread (Matt. 4:4), meat (Heb. 5:11–14), and even honey (Ps. 119:103). Just as the physical man needs a balanced diet if his body is to be healthy, so the inner man needs a balanced diet of spiritual food. The baby begins with milk, but as he grows and his teeth develop, he needs solid food.

It is not difficult to determine a believer's spiritual maturity, or immaturity, if you discover what kind of "diet" he enjoys. The immature believer knows little about the present ministry of Christ in heaven. He knows the *facts* about our Lord's life and ministry on earth, but not the *truths* about His present ministry in heaven. He lives on "Bible stories" and not Bible doctrines. He has no understanding of 1 Corinthians 2:6–7.

In my itinerant ministry, I have preached in hundreds of churches and conferences; and I have always been grateful for congregations that wanted to be enlightened and edified, not entertained. It is important that we preach the gospel to the lost; but it is also important that we *interpret* the gospel to the saved. The entire New Testament is an interpretation and application of the gospel. Paul did not write Romans, for example, to tell the Romans how to be saved—for they were already saints. He wrote to explain to them what was really involved in their salvation. It was an explanation of the "deep things of God" and how they applied to daily life.

There is another way to determine maturity: The mature Christian practices love and seeks to get along with others. Children like to disagree and fuss. And children like to identify with heroes, whether sports heroes or Hollywood heroes. The "babes" in Corinth were fighting over which preacher was the greatest—Paul, Apollos, or Peter. It sounded like children on the playground: "My father can fight better than your father! My father makes more money than your father!"

When immature Christians, without spiritual discernment, get into places of leadership in the church, the results will be disastrous. More than one brokenhearted pastor has phoned me, or written me, asking what to do with church officers who talk big but live small. (In all fairness, I should say that sometimes it is the *officers* who write asking what to do with an immature pastor!)

The work of the pastor is to help the church grow spiritually and mature in the Lord. This is done by the steady, balanced ministry of the Word. Ephesians 4:1–16 explains how this is done: It is necessary for each member of the body to make his own contribution. God gives spiritual gifts to His people, and then He gives these gifted people to the various churches to build up the saints. As the believers grow, they build the church.

Paul will have more to say about spiritual gifts in 1 Corinthians 12—14, but this should be said now: A mature Christian uses his gifts as tools to build with, while an immature believer uses gifts as toys to play with or trophies to boast about. Many of the members of the Corinthian church enjoyed "showing off" their gifts, but they were not interested in serving one another and edifying the church.

What is the ministry all about? It involves loving, feeding, and disciplining God's family so that His children mature in the faith and become more like Jesus Christ.

2. THE FIELD—QUANTITY (3:5–9A)

Paul was fond of agricultural images and often used them in his letters. "Ye are God's husbandry" simply means, "You are God's cultivated field, God's garden." In the parable of the sower, Jesus compared the human heart to soil and the Word of God to seed (Matt. 13:1–9, 18–23). Paul took this *individual* image and made it *collective:* The local church is a field that ought to bear fruit. The task of the ministry is the sowing of the seed, the cultivating of the soil, the watering of the plants, and the harvesting of the fruit.

How did this image of the church as a "field" apply to the special problems of the Corinthians? To begin with, the emphasis must be on God and not on the laborers. Paul and Apollos were only servants who did their assigned tasks. It was God who gave life to their efforts. Even the faith of the believers was a gift from God (1 Cor. 3:5). It is wrong to center attention on the servants. Look instead to the Lord of the harvest, the source of all blessing.

Note the emphasis in this paragraph on *increase* or *growth*. Why compare preachers or statistics? God is the source of the growth; no man can take the credit. Furthermore, no one man can do *all* the necessary work. Paul planted the seed, Apollos watered it, but only God could make it grow (1 Cor. 3:6).

Three main lessons appear from this image.

First, diversity of ministry. One laborer plows the soil, another sows the seed, a third waters the seed. As time passes, the plants grow, the fruit appears, and other laborers enjoy reaping the harvest. This emphasis on diversity will also show up when Paul compares the church to a body with many different parts.

Second, unity of purpose. No matter what work a person is doing for the Lord, he is still a part of the harvest. "Now he that planteth and he that watereth are one" (1 Cor. 3:8). Paul, Apollos, and Peter were not competing with each other. Rather, each was doing his assigned task under the lordship of Jesus Christ. Even though there is diversity of ministry, there is unity of purpose; and there ought to be unity of spirit.

Third, humility of spirit. It is not the human laborers who produce the harvest, but the Lord of the harvest. "God gave the increase.… God that giveth the increase" (1 Cor. 3:6–7). Granted, God has ordained that human beings should be His ministers on earth; but their efforts apart from God's blessing would be failures. The Corinthians were proud of their church, and various groups in the assembly were proud of their leaders. But this attitude of being "puffed up" was dividing the church because God was not receiving the glory.

Jesus expressed the same idea as recorded in John 4:34–38. The sower and the reaper not only work together, but one day they shall rejoice together and receive their own rewards. There can be no such thing as isolated ministry, because each worker enters into the labors of others. I have had the privilege of leading people to Christ who were total strangers to me, but others had sown the seed and watered it with their love and prayers.

"And every man shall receive his own reward according to his own labour" (1 Cor. 3:8). What men may think of our ministry is not important; what God may think is of supreme importance. Our reward must not be the praise of men, but the "Well done!" of the Lord of the harvest.

God wants to see increase in His field. He wants each local church to produce the fruit of the Spirit (Gal. 5:22–23), holiness (Rom. 6:22), giving (Rom. 15:26), good works (Col. 1:10), praise to the Lord (Heb. 13:15), and souls won to Christ (Rom. 1:13). Along with spiritual growth, there should be a measure of numerical growth. *Fruit has in it the seed for more fruit.* If the fruit of our ministry is genuine, it will eventually produce "more fruit … much fruit" to the glory of God (John 15:1–8).

Those who serve in ministry must constantly be caring for the "soil" of the church. It requires diligence and hard work to produce a harvest. The lazy preacher or Sunday school teacher is like the slothful farmer Solomon wrote about in Proverbs 24:30–34. Satan is busy sowing discord, lies, and sin; and we must be busy cultivating the soil and planting the good seed of the Word of God.

3. The Temple—Quality (3:9b–23)

The usual explanation of this passage is that it describes the building of the Christian life. We all build on Christ, but some people use good materials, while others use poor materials. The kind of material you use determines the kind of reward you will get.

While this may be a valid *application* of this passage, it is not the basic *interpretation*. Paul was discussing the building of the local church, the temple of God. (In 1 Corinthians 6:19–20, the individual believer is God's temple; but here it is the local assembly that is in view. In Eph. 2:19–22, the whole church is compared to a temple of God.) Paul pointed out that one day God will judge our labors as related to the local assembly. "The fire will test the quality of each man's work" (1 Cor. 3:13 NIV).

God is concerned that we build with quality. The church does not belong to the preacher or to the congregation. It is *God's* church. "Ye are God's building" (1 Cor. 3:9). If we are going to build the local church the way God wants it built, we must meet certain conditions.

First, we must build on the right foundation (vv. 10–11). That foundation is Jesus Christ. When Paul came to Corinth, he determined to preach only Christ and Him crucified (1 Cor. 2:1–2). He laid the only foundation that would last. In more than thirty years of ministry, I have seen "churches" try to build on a famous preacher or a special method or a doctrinal emphasis they felt was important; but these ministries simply did not last. The Corinthians were emphasizing personalities—Paul, Peter, Apollos—when they should have been glorifying Christ.

The foundation is laid by the proclaiming of the gospel of Jesus Christ. The foundation is the most important part of the building, because it determines the size, shape, and strength of the superstructure. A ministry may seem to be successful for a time, but if it is not founded on Christ, it will eventually collapse and disappear.

I am thinking now of a pastor who "discovered a great truth" in the Bible (actually, he read it in some books) and decided to build his church on the promotion of that "great truth." He split his church and took a group with him who were "devoted to the truth" he had discovered. But the new church never succeeded. Now his group is scattered and he goes from church to church, trying to get converts to his cause. He built on the wrong foundation.

Gold, Silver, Precious Stones	Wood, Hay, Stubble
Permanent	Passing, temporary
Beautiful	Ordinary, even ugly
Valuable	Cheap
Hard to obtain	Easy to obtain

Second, we must build with the right materials (vv. 12–17). Paul described two opposite kinds of materials, as the chart reveals.

What did Paul want to symbolize by his choice of materials? He was not talking about *people,* because Christians are the "living stones" that make up God's temple (1 Peter 2:5). I personally believe Paul was referring to the *doctrines of the Word of God.* In each section of this chapter, the Word is symbolized in a way that fits the image of the church Paul used. The Word is food for the family, seed for the field, and materials for the temple.

The book of Proverbs presents the wisdom of the Word of God as treasure to be sought, protected, and invested in daily life. Consider these passages:

Happy is the man that findeth wisdom, and the man that getteth understanding. For the merchandise of it is better than the merchandise of silver, and the gain thereof than fine gold. She is more precious than rubies. (3:13–15a)

My son, if thou wilt receive my words, and hide my commandments with thee; so that thou incline thine ear unto wisdom, and apply thine heart to understanding; yea, if thou criest after knowledge, and liftest up thy voice for understanding; if thou seekest her as silver, and searchest for

her as for hid treasures; then shalt thou understand the fear of
the LORD, and find the knowledge of God. (2:1–5)

Receive my instruction, and not silver; and knowledge rather
than choice gold. For wisdom is better than rubies; and all
the things that may be desired are not to be compared to it.
(8:10–11)

When you remember that Paul has been writing about *wisdom* in these
first three chapters, you can easily see the connection. The Corinthians
were trying to build their church by man's wisdom, the wisdom of this
world, when they should have been depending on the wisdom of God
as found in the Word.

This says to me that ministers of the Word must dig deep into the
Scriptures and mine out the precious gold, silver, and jewels, and then
build these truths into the lives of the people. D. L. Moody used to say
that converts should be weighed as well as counted. God is interested in
quality as well as *quantity,* and Paul made it clear that it is possible to
have both. The faithful minister can work in the field and see increase,
and he can build with the Word of God and see beauty and lasting
blessings.

It is a serious thing to be a part of the building of God's temple.
First Corinthians 3:16–17 warns us that if we destroy ("defile") God's
temple by using cheap materials, God will destroy us! This does not
mean eternal condemnation, of course, because 1 Corinthians 3:15
assures us that each worker will be saved, even if he loses a reward. I
think Paul is saying that each of us builds into the church *what we build
into our own lives.* Veteran missionary to India Amy Carmichael used to
say, "The work will never go deeper than we have gone ourselves." So we
end up tearing down our own lives if we fail to build into the church the

values that will last. We may look very successful to men, but "the day shall declare it," and on that day, some ministers will go up in smoke.

It is unwise to compare and contrast ministries. Paul warned in 1 Corinthians 4:5, "Therefore judge nothing before the time."

Young ministers often asked Dr. Campbell Morgan the secret of his pulpit success. Morgan replied, "I always say to them the same thing—work; hard work; and again, work!" Morgan was in his study at six o'clock each morning, digging treasures out of the Bible. You can find wood, hay, and stubble in your backyard, and it will not take too much effort to pick it up. But if you want gold, silver, and jewels, *you have to dig for them.* Lazy preachers and Sunday school teachers will have much to answer for at the judgment seat of Christ—and so will preachers and teachers who *steal* materials from others instead of studying and making it their own.

Third, we must build according to the right plan (vv. 18–20). It comes as a shock to some church members that you cannot manage a local church the same way you run a business. This does not mean we should not follow good business principles, but the operation is totally different. There is a wisdom of this world that works for the world, but it will not work for the church.

The world depends on promotion, prestige, and the influence of money and important people. The church depends on prayer, the power of the Spirit, humility, sacrifice, and service. The church that imitates the world may seem to succeed in time, but it will turn to ashes in eternity. The church in the book of Acts had none of the "secrets of success" that seem to be important today. They owned no property; they had no influence in government; they had no treasury ("Silver and gold have I none," said Peter); their leaders were ordinary men without special education in the accepted schools; they held no attendance contests; they brought in no celebrities; and yet they turned the world upside down!

God has a specific plan for each local church (Phil. 2:12–13). Each pastor and church leader must seek the mind of God for His wisdom. First Corinthians 3:19 warns that man's wisdom will only trap him (a quotation from Job 5:13); and 1 Corinthians 3:20 warns that man's wisdom only leads to vanity and futility (a quotation from Ps. 94:11). Though the church must be identified with the *needs* of the world, it must not imitate the *wisdom* of the world.

Finally, we must build with the right motive (vv. 21–23). That motive is the glory of God. The members of the Corinthian church were glorying in men, and this was wrong. They were comparing men (1 Cor. 4:6) and dividing the church by such carnal deeds. Had they been seeking to glorify God alone, there would have been harmony in the assembly.

Paul closed this appeal by pointing out that each believer possesses all things in Christ. Each one of God's servants belongs to *each* believer. No member of the church should say, "I belong to Paul!" or "I like Peter!" because each servant belongs to each member equally. Perhaps we cannot help but have our personal preferences when it comes to the way different men minister the Word. But we must not permit our personal preferences to become divisive prejudices. In fact, the preacher I may enjoy the least may be the one I need the most!

"All are yours"—the world, life, death, things present, things to come! How rich we are in Christ! If all things belong to all believers, then why should there be competition and rivalry? "Get your eyes off of men!" Paul admonished. "Keep your eyes on Christ, and work with Him in building the church!"

"Ye are Christ's"—this balances things. I have all things in Jesus Christ, but I must not become careless or use my freedom unwisely. "All things are yours"—that is Christian *liberty*. "And ye are Christ's"—that is Christian *responsibility*. We need both if we are to build a church that will not turn to ashes when the fire falls.

How we need to pray for ministers of the Word! They must feed the family and bring the children to maturity. They must sow the seed in the field and pray for an increase. They must mine the treasures of the Word and build these treasures into the temple. No wonder Paul cried, "And who is sufficient for these things?" But he also gave the answer: "Our sufficiency is of God" (2 Cor. 2:16; 3:5).

QUESTIONS FOR PERSONAL REFLECTION
OR GROUP DISCUSSION

1. If the church were like your natural family, what would be some of its characteristics?

2. How is the church like a family? A field? A temple?

3. What are some marks of spiritual maturity?

4. What did Paul mean when he said that the Corinthians were fleshly or worldly?

5. Though one legitimate goal of ministry is numerical growth, competition sometimes arises. How can competition among ministries be prevented?

6. Why is it essential that the church have diversity of ministries?

7. Why is it essential that the church have unity of purpose?

8. In 3:6, Paul says the temple of God's Spirit is "you" plural, not you as an individual. What is the significance of this?

9. Wiersbe states, "You cannot manage a local church the same way you run a business." How are a church and a business different?

10. What practical wisdom for participating in a church have you gained from 1 Corinthians 3?

Chapter Four

BE WISE ABOUT THE CHRISTIAN MINISTRY

(1 Corinthians 4)

In 1 Corinthians 3, Paul presented three pictures of the local church. Now he presents three pictures of the minister—a steward (1 Cor. 4:1–6), a spectacle (1 Cor. 4:7–13), and a father (1 Cor. 4:14–21). He wanted his readers to understand how God measures and evaluates a Christian's service. First Corinthians 4:6 explains Paul's purpose: "That no one of you be puffed up for one against another."

We must avoid extremes when it comes to evaluating men and their ministries. On the one hand, we can be so indifferent that we accept anybody who comes along. But the other extreme is to be so hypercritical that Paul himself would fail the test. It is important that we "try the spirits" (1 John 4:1–6; 2 John), but we must be careful not to grieve the Spirit as we do so.

In these three pictures of ministry, Paul presented three characteristics of a true minister of Jesus Christ.

1. FAITHFULNESS: THE STEWARD (4:1–6)

Paul answered the leaders of the various factions in the church when he called himself, Peter, and Apollos "ministers of Christ." The word translated "ministers" is literally "under-rowers." It described the slaves who rowed the huge Roman galleys. "We are not the captains of the ship," said Paul, "but only the galley slaves who are under orders. Now, is one slave greater than another?"

Then Paul explained the image of the *steward*. A steward is a servant who manages everything for his master, but who himself owns nothing. Joseph was a chief steward in Potiphar's household (Gen. 39). The church is the "household of faith" (Gal. 6:10), and the ministers are stewards who share God's wealth with the family (Matt. 13:52). Paul called this spiritual wealth "the mysteries of God." We met this important word *mystery* in 1 Corinthians 2:7, so you may want to review it.

The responsibility of the steward is to be *faithful to his master*. A steward may not please the members of the household; he may not even please some of the other servants; but if he pleases his own master, he is a good steward. This same idea is expressed in Romans 14:4.

So, the main issue is not, "Is Paul popular?" or, "Is Apollos a better preacher than Paul?" The main issue is, "Have Paul, Apollos, and Peter been faithful to do the work God assigned to them?" Jesus had this same test in mind when He told the parable recorded in Luke 12:41–48. If a servant of God is faithful in his personal life, in his home, and in his ministry of the Word, then he is a good steward and will be adequately rewarded.

But a servant is constantly being judged. There is always somebody criticizing something he does. Paul pointed out that there are three judgments in the life of the steward.

(1) There is man's judgment (v. 3a). Paul did not get upset when people criticized him, for he knew that his Master's judgment was far more important. The phrase *man's judgment* is literally "man's day." This is in contrast to *God's* day of judgment yet to come (1 Cor. 1:8; 3:13).

(2) There is the servant's own self-judgment (vv. 3b–4a). Paul knew nothing that was amiss in his life and ministry, but even that did not excuse him. Sometimes we do not really know ourselves. There can be a fine line between a clear conscience and a self-righteous attitude, so we must beware.

(3) The most important judgment is God's judgment (v. 4b). Certainly God judges us today through His Word (Heb. 4:12) and by the ministry of the Spirit. Sometimes He uses the ministry of a loving friend to help us face and confess sin (Matt. 18:15–17). But the main reference here is to the final evaluation when each Christian stands at the judgment seat of Christ (Rom. 14:10; 2 Cor. 5:10). Then the true facts will be revealed and the faithful servants rewarded.

These verses must not be used to cultivate a self-righteous independence of people. The local church is a family, and members of the family must help each other to grow. There is a place for honest, loving criticism (Eph. 4:15). If the critic is right, then he has helped us. If he is wrong, then we can help him. Either way, the truth is strengthened.

Paul's "therefore" in 1 Corinthians 4:5 alerts us that he is about to make a personal application of the truths just discussed. He closed this section with a threefold rebuke.

First, you are judging God's servants at the wrong time (v. 5). It is when the Lord returns that He will evaluate their lives and ministries, so wait until then. In fact, you cannot see into men's hearts; you cannot begin to judge their motives. Only God can do that. "Man looketh on the outward appearance, but the LORD looketh on the heart" (1 Sam. 16:7).

The Corinthians who were passing judgment on Paul were actually "playing God" and assuming to themselves the privileges that only God has. How often in my own ministry I have made this mistake! How easy it is to misread a situation and misjudge a person.

Second, you are judging by the wrong standard (v. 6a). The Corinthians were measuring different men by their own personal preferences and prejudices. They were even comparing ministers with one another. The only true basis for evaluation is "that which is written"—the Word of God.

The Bible clearly reveals what kind of life and service is required of God's ministers. There is no need for us to devise new standards. Often I receive letters from churches seeking pastors, asking if I could recommend candidates to them. Too often their "requirements" have gone beyond what God requires in His Word. Again, it is the problem Paul discussed in 1 Corinthians 1 and 2—the wisdom of men versus the wisdom of God.

Third, you are judging with the wrong motive (v. 6b). Each group in the church was tearing down the other preachers in order to build up the man they liked. Their motive was not at all spiritual. They were promoting division in the church by being partisan to one man as opposed to the others. They needed to examine their own hearts and get rid of the pride that was destroying the church.

God's servants are stewards of His truth, and the key test is, *Have they been faithful to obey and to teach the Word of God?* Not just faithful *preaching,* but faithful *practicing* as well. The testimony of Samuel (1 Sam. 12:1–5) and Paul (Acts 20:17ff.) will bear witness to this truth.

2. HUMBLENESS: THE SPECTACLE (4:7–13)

When Paul called himself and other apostles "a spectacle unto the world" (1 Cor. 4:9), he was using an image familiar to people in the Roman Empire. The government kept the people pacified by presenting entertainments in the different cities. The amphitheaters would be filled with citizens, eager to see men compete in the games and prisoners fight with the beasts. (In fact, the Greek word translated "spectacle" gives us our English word *theater.*) The Coliseum at Rome became the center for these "entertainments."

When the "main events" were ended, then the poorest and weakest prisoners were brought in to fight with the beasts. Nobody expected too much from their performance.

What a picture of the apostles of Jesus Christ! But it forms the background for a series of contrasts that Paul presented for the purpose of trying to humble the Corinthians.

Kings—prisoners (vv. 7–9). The questions in 1 Corinthians 4:7 ought to make all of us stop and think. I like the New American Standard Bible's translation of the first question: "Who regards you as superior?" A young preacher once said to a friend of mine, "Please pray that I will stay humble." My friend replied, "Tell me, what do you have to be proud about?" Why would anybody regard us as superior? Perhaps it is our own biased opinion that makes us feel so important. The best commentary on 1 Corinthians 4:7 is the witness of John the Baptist: "A man can receive nothing, except it be given him from heaven.… He [Christ] must increase, but I must decrease" (John 3:27, 30).

Paul used a bit of sanctified sarcasm in 1 Corinthians 4:8 when he described the Corinthians as kings. "I wish I could reign with you and be important!" he wrote. "But instead, I must go into the arena and suffer for the Lord Jesus Christ. You are first in men's eyes, but we apostles are last." In the eyes of God, the apostles were first (1 Cor. 12:28), but in the eyes of men they were last.

There is no place for pride in the ministry. If a truly great leader like Paul considered himself "on exhibition last in the program," where does this leave the rest of us? Church members are wrong when they measure ministers other than by the standards God has given. They are also wrong when they boast about their favorite preachers. This is not to say that faithful servants cannot be recognized and honored, but in all things God must be glorified (1 Thess. 5:12–13).

Wise men—fools (v. 10a). Paul was a fool according to the standards of men. Had he remained a Jewish rabbi, he could have attained great heights in the Jewish religion (Gal. 1:14). Or had he sided with the Jewish legalists in the Jerusalem church and not ministered to the Gentiles, he could have avoided a great deal of persecution (Acts 15; 21:17ff.). But when Paul asked the Lord, "What wilt thou have me to do?" (Acts 9:6) he really meant it.

The Corinthians were wise in their own eyes, but they were actually fools in the sight of God. By depending on the wisdom and the standards of the world, they were acting like fools. The way to be spiritually wise is to become a fool in the eyes of the world (1 Cor. 3:18). I often find myself quoting these words of martyred Jim Elliot: "He is no fool who gives what he cannot keep to gain what he cannot lose."

Strong men—weak (v. 10b). There was a time when Paul gloried in his strengths; but then he met Jesus Christ and discovered that what he thought were assets were really liabilities (Phil. 3). It was through his own personal suffering that Paul discovered that his spiritual strength was the result of personal weakness (2 Cor. 12:7–10). Strength that knows itself to be strength is weakness; but weakness that knows itself to be weakness becomes strength.

The Corinthians were proud of their spiritual achievements. The factions in the church were proud of their human leaders and favorite preachers. But all of this was only weakness. There is strength only when God gets the glory. "My strength is made perfect in weakness" (2 Cor. 12:9).

Honorable—despised (vv. 10c–13). This was the crux of the whole matter: The Christians in Corinth wanted the honor that comes from men, not the honor that comes from God. They were trying to "borrow" glory by associating themselves with "great men." Paul answered, "If you associate with us, you had better be ready for suffering. We apostles are not held in honor—we are despised!"

Paul then described the privations and sufferings that he had to endure as a servant of God. The fact that he worked with his own hands as a tentmaker would have lowered him in the eyes of many, because the Greeks despised manual labor.

Paul also described how he responded to the way people treated him; and this, in itself, helped to make him great. What life does to us depends on what life finds in us. When Paul was reviled, he blessed—just as Jesus commanded (Matt. 5:44). When persecuted, he endured it by the grace of God and did not retaliate. When he was slandered, Paul tried to conciliate. In all things, he sought to respond in love.

What was the result? Men treated him "as the filth of the world … the offscouring of all things" (1 Cor. 4:13). "Away with such a fellow from the earth: for it is not fit that he should live" (Acts 22:22). Paul and the other apostles were treated just as their Lord was treated; but God vindicated them and brought glory to His name.

Faithfulness in service and humbleness of mind: These are two important characteristics of a minister of Jesus Christ. He must be willing to work and willing to suffer. It is one thing to be faithful and quite another to be popular. But there is a third characteristic that helps to balance the others.

3. TENDERNESS: THE FATHER (4:14–21)

Paul had already compared the local church to a family (1 Cor. 3:1–4). But now the emphasis is on the minister as a "spiritual father." In none of his letters did Paul ever call himself "father." He was mindful of the Lord's teaching in Matthew 23:8–12. But in comparing himself to a "spiritual father," Paul reminded the church of the important ministries he had performed on their behalf.

First, Paul had founded the family (vv. 14–15). The Corinthians were Paul's beloved children in the faith. Whenever we share the gospel with someone and have the joy of leading him to faith in Christ, we become a "spiritual parent" in his life. This does not give us any special authority over his faith (2 Cor. 1:24), but it *does* create a special relationship that God can use to help him grow. The local church is God's family for helping the newborn Christians develop.

It is important to note that Paul did not take the credit for their conversion. Their spiritual birth was *in Christ* and *through the gospel.*

Sinners are born again through the ministry of the Spirit of God and the Word of God (John 3:6; 1 Peter 1:23–25). Paul was the "father" who stood by and assisted at their birth.

A child may have many guardians and teachers, but he can have only one father. He has a special relationship to his father that must not be preempted by anyone else. There had been no church in Corinth before Paul came, so that even the second-generation believers in the church were the results of Paul's effective ministry.

Paul founded the church and Apollos followed him and taught the people. In some way that is not made clear in the Scriptures, Peter also ministered at Corinth. (Perhaps he had not been there personally, but other teachers from Jerusalem had ministered in Corinth as "representatives" of Peter.) God's children need the ministry of different teachers, but they must never forget the "spiritual father" who brought them to Christ.

Second, Paul was an example to the family (vv. 16–17). Children have a way of imitating their parents, either for good or for ill. Researchers tell us that teenagers learn to drink at home and not from their peers. My guess is that other bad habits are learned the same way.

The word *followers* literally means "mimics." Paul gave the same admonition in Philippians 3:17, but we must not think that he was exalting himself. Little children learn first by example, then by explanation. When Paul pastored the church in Corinth, he set the example before them in love, devotion to Christ, sacrifice, and service. "Be ye followers of me, even as I also am of Christ" (1 Cor. 11:1). Paul was a good example because he was following the greatest Example of all, Jesus Christ.

But Paul was also a good teacher. It takes both example and instruction to bring a child to maturity. Paul sent Timothy (also one of his spiritual children) to remind the church of the doctrines and practices that Paul always taught. Timothy did not carry the letter to the church (1 Cor. 16:10), but apparently went ahead to prepare the way for the letter.

God does not have one standard for one church and a different standard for another church. He may work out His will in different ways (Phil. 2:12–13), but the basic doctrines and principles are the same. Because churches have gotten away from God's wisdom and have substituted man's wisdom, we have serious doctrinal differences among various churches. Men have gone beyond "that which is written" (1 Cor. 4:6), and this has brought division into the church.

Third, Paul was faithful to discipline the family (vv. 18–21). A child's will must be broken, but not destroyed. Until a colt is broken, it is dangerous and useless; but once it learns to obey, it becomes gentle and useful. Pride is a terrible thing in the Christian life and in the church. The yeast of sin (leaven, 1 Cor. 5:6–8) had made the Corinthians "puffed up," even to the point of saying, "Paul will not come to us! His bark is worse than his bite!" (2 Cor. 10:8–11).

Paul had been patient with their disobedience, but now he warned them that the time had come for discipline. Paul was not like the tolerant modern mother who shouted at her spoiled son, "This is the last time I'm going to tell you for the last time!"

A faithful parent must discipline his children. It is not enough to teach them and be an example before them; he must also punish them when they rebel and refuse to obey. Paul would have preferred to come with meekness and deal with their sins in a gentle manner, but their own attitude made this difficult. They were puffed up—and even proud of their disobedience (1 Cor. 5:1–2)!

The contrast in this paragraph is between *speech* and *power*, words and deeds. The arrogant Corinthians had no problem "talking big," the way children often will do; but they could not back up their talk with their "walk." Their religion was only in words. Paul was prepared to back up his talk with power, with deeds that would reveal their sins and God's holiness.

This section prepared the way for the next two chapters that deal with discipline in the local church. There was much sin in the Corinthian congregation, and Paul was prepared to deal with it. He had already written them a letter about the matter (1 Cor. 5:9), but the congregation had not obeyed him. It was then that some of the more spiritual members contacted Paul (1 Cor. 1:11; 16:17) and shared the burdens with him. Some of the church leaders had written Paul for counsel (1 Cor. 7:1), and Paul prayed that they might obey the counsel he wrote to them.

It is a principle of life that those who will not govern themselves must be governed. Insurance companies and medical authorities urged drivers to wear seat belts, but many of them refused. So the government passed a law *requiring* drivers to wear seat belts. If you fail to obey, you will be punished.

Paul gave the Corinthian church the opportunity to set their household in order. In the following chapters, he explained how the local church ought to be governed in the will of God. Unfortunately, the church did not immediately obey. Paul had to make a quick visit to Corinth, and his experience during that visit was very painful (2 Cor. 2:1; 12:14; 13:1). He then had to write them a very strong letter (1 Cor. 7:8–12); possibly it was carried by Titus.

To the glory of God, the matters did get settled for the most part. There was still some mopping up to do (2 Cor. 12:20—13:5), but the crisis was now over.

It is not an easy thing to be a minister of Jesus Christ. As a steward, you must be faithful to your Master no matter what men may say to you or do to you. You will be treated as refuse by the people of the world. Your own spiritual children may break your heart and have to be disciplined.

God's faithful servants deserve our love, respect, obedience, and prayer support.

QUESTIONS FOR PERSONAL REFLECTION
OR GROUP DISCUSSION

1. What qualities do you think most Christians look for in a leader?

2. What is a steward?

3. Why is it important that stewards be faithful?

4. According to Paul in 4:1–7, what are some wrong approaches to evaluating or judging the work of church leaders? What might be a right approach?

5. Why is it dangerous for us to judge ourselves? In what ways does God judge us?

6. What is the key test for God's ministers (4:5)?

7. What did Paul mean by "spectacle" in 4:9? What does this imagery say about the nature of true Christian leadership?

8. How does a father show tenderness to his children?

9. In what way was Paul like a father to the Corinthian church? In what way were the Corinthians like children?

10. How would you like to relate to church leaders—or be a church leader—in light of 1 Corinthians 4?

Chapter Five

BE WISE ABOUT CHURCH DISCIPLINE

(1 Corinthians 5—6)

The church at Corinth was not only a divided church, but it was also a disgraced church. There was sin in the assembly and, sad to say, everybody knew about it. But the church was slow to *do* anything about it.

No church is perfect, but human imperfection must never be an excuse for sin. Just as parents must discipline their children in love, so local churches must exercise discipline over the members of the assembly. Church discipline is not a group of "pious policemen" out to catch a criminal. Rather, it is a group of brokenhearted brothers and sisters seeking to restore an erring member of the family.

Since some of the members at Corinth did not want to face the situation and change it, Paul presented to the church three important considerations.

1. CONSIDER THE CHURCH (5:1–13)

"What will this sin do to the church?" is certainly an important consideration. Christians are "called to be saints" (1 Cor. 1:2), and this means holy living to the glory of God. If a Christian loves his church, he will not stand by and permit sin to weaken it and perhaps ruin its testimony.

How should we respond? Paul gave three specific instructions for the church to follow.

(1) Mourn over the sin (vv. 1–2). This is the word used for mourning over the dead, which is perhaps the deepest and most painful kind of personal sorrow possible. Instead of mourning, the people at Corinth were puffed up. They were boasting of the fact that their church was so "open-minded" that even fornicators could be members in good standing!

The sin in question was a form of incest: A professed Christian (and a member of the church) was living with his stepmother in a permanent alliance. Since Paul does not pass judgment on the woman (1 Cor. 5:9–13), we assume that she was not a member of the assembly and probably not even a Christian. This kind of sin was condemned by the Old Testament law (Lev. 18:6–8; 20:11) as well as by the laws of the Gentile nations. Paul shamed the church by saying, "Even the unsaved Gentiles don't practice this kind of sin!"

While it is true that the Christian life is a feast (1 Cor. 5:8), there are times when it becomes a funeral. Whenever a Christian brother or sister sins, it is time for the family to mourn and to seek to help the fallen believer (Gal. 6:1–2). The offending brother in Corinth was "dead" as far as the things of the Lord were concerned. He was out of fellowship with the Lord and with those in the church who were living separated lives.

(2) Judge the sin (vv. 3–5). While Christians are not to judge one another's motives (Matt. 7:1–5) or ministries (1 Cor. 4:5), we are certainly expected to be honest about each other's conduct. In my own pastoral ministry, I have never enjoyed having to initiate church discipline; but since it is commanded in the Scriptures, we must obey God and set personal feelings aside.

Paul described here an official church meeting at which the offender was dealt with according to divine instructions. Public sin must be publicly judged and condemned. (For our Lord's instructions about discipline, study Matt. 18:15–20.) The sin was not to be swept under the rug; for, after all, it was known far and wide even among the unsaved who were outside the church.

The church was to gather together and expel the offender. Note the strong words that Paul used to instruct them: "taken away from among you" (1 Cor. 5:2), "deliver such an one unto Satan" (1 Cor. 5:5), "purge out" (1 Cor. 5:7), and "put away" (1 Cor. 5:13). Paul did not suggest that they handle the offender gently. Of course, we assume that first the spiritual leaders of the church sought to restore the man personally.

This was to be done by the authority of Jesus Christ—in His name—and not simply on the authority of the local church. Church membership is a serious thing and must not be treated carelessly or lightly.

What does it mean to deliver a Christian "unto Satan"? It does not mean to deprive him of salvation, since it is not the church that grants salvation to begin with. When a Christian is in fellowship with the Lord and with the local church, he enjoys a special protection from Satan. But when he is out of fellowship with God and excommunicated from the local church, he is "fair game" for the enemy. God could permit Satan to attack the offender's body so that the sinning believer would repent and return to the Lord.

(3) Purge the sin (vv. 6–13). The image here is that of the Passover supper (Ex. 12). Jesus is the Lamb of God who shed His blood to deliver us from sin (John 1:29; 1 Peter 1:18–25). The Jews in Egypt were delivered from death by the application of the blood of the lamb. Following the application of the blood, the Jewish families ate the Passover supper. One of the requirements was that no yeast (leaven) be found anywhere in their dwellings. Even the bread at the feast was to be unleavened.

Leaven is a picture of sin. It is small but powerful; it works secretly; it "puffs up" the dough; it spreads. The sinning church member in Corinth was like a piece of yeast: He was defiling the entire loaf of bread (the congregation). It was like a cancer in the body that needed to be removed by drastic surgery.

The church must purge itself of "old leaven"—the things that belong to the "old life" before we trusted Christ. We must also get rid of malice and wickedness (there was a great deal of hard feelings between members of the Corinthian church) and replace them with sincerity and truth. As a loaf of bread (1 Cor. 10:17), the local church must be as pure as possible.

However, the church must not judge and condemn those who are *outside* the faith. That judgment is future, and God will take care of it. In 1 Corinthians 5:9–13, Paul emphasized once again the importance of separation from the world. Christians are not to be *isolated,* but separated. We cannot avoid contact with sinners, but we can avoid contamination by sinners.

If a professed Christian is guilty of the sins named here, the church must deal with him. Individual members are not to "company" with him (1 Cor. 5:9—"get mixed up with, associate intimately"). They are not to *eat* with him, which could refer to private hospitality or more likely the public observance of the Lord's Supper (1 Cor. 11:23–34).

Church discipline is not easy or popular, but it is important. If it is done properly, God can use it to convict and restore an erring believer. Second Corinthians 2:1–11 indicates that this man did repent and was restored to fellowship.

2. Consider Lost Sinners (1–8)

The church at Corinth was rapidly losing its testimony in the city. Not only did the unsaved know about the immorality in the assembly, but they were also aware of the lawsuits involving members of the church. Not only were there sins of the flesh, but also sins of the spirit (2 Cor. 7:1).

The Greeks in general, and the Athenians in particular, were known for their involvement in the courts. The Greek playwright Aristophanes has one of his characters look at a map and ask where Greece is located. When it is pointed out to him, he replies that there must be some mistake—because he cannot see any lawsuits going on! However, the United States is rapidly getting a similar reputation: Over two hundred thousand civil suits were filed in the federal courts in one recent twelve-month period. Nearly one million lawyers (their number is increasing) are handling them. In one year, more than twelve million suits were filed in the state courts.

Paul detected three tragedies in this situation.

First, the believers were presenting a poor testimony to the lost. Even the unbelieving Jews dealt with their civil cases in their own synagogue courts. To take the problems of Christians and discuss them before the "unjust" and "unbelievers" was to weaken the testimony of the gospel.

Second, the congregation had failed to live up to its full position in Christ. Since the saints will one day participate in the judgment of the world and even of fallen angels, they ought to be able to settle their differences here on earth. The Corinthians boasted of their great spiritual gifts. Why, then, did they not use them in solving their problems?

Bible students are not agreed on the meaning of Paul's statement in 1 Corinthians 6:4. Some think he is using a bit of sarcasm: "You are better off asking the weakest member of your church to settle the matter, than to go before the most qualified unsaved judge!" Others take the phrase "who are least esteemed in [or 'by'] the church" to refer to the pagan judges. Or it may be that Paul is saying that God can use even the least member of the church to discern His will. The result is still the same: It is wrong for Christians to take their civil suits to court.

Sometimes there are "friendly suits" that are required by law to settle certain issues. That is not what Paul was referring to. It seems that the church members were at each other's throats, trying to get their way in the courts. I am happy to see that there is a trend in our churches today for

Christian lawyers to act as arbitrators in civil cases and help to settle these matters out of court.

There was a third tragedy: The members suing each other had already lost. Even if some of them won their cases, they had incurred a far greater loss in their disobedience to the Word of God. "Now therefore there is utterly a fault among you" (1 Cor. 6:7) can be translated, "It is already a complete defeat for you." Paul was certainly referring to our Lord's teaching in Matthew 5:39–42. Better to lose money or possessions than to lose a brother and lose your testimony as well.

Over the years of my own ministry, I have seen the sad results of churches and church members trying to solve personal problems in court. Nobody really wins—except the Devil! The Corinthians who were going to court were disgracing the name of the Lord and the church just as much as the man who was guilty of incest, and they needed to be disciplined.

I recall a ministerial student who phoned me to tell me he was going to sue his school. Apparently the administration would not allow him to do something he felt was very necessary to his education. I advised him to cool off, talk to his faculty counselor, and get the idea out of his mind. He took my advice and in so doing not only avoided a bad testimony, but grew spiritually through the experience.

3. CONSIDER THE LORD (6:9–20)

There was a great deal of sexual laxness in the city of Corinth. It was a permissive society with a philosophy similar to that which the world has today: Sex is a normal physical function, so why not use it as you please? Paul pointed out that God created sex when He made the first man and woman, and therefore He has the right to tell us how to use it. The Bible is the "owner's manual," and it must be obeyed.

God condemns sexual sins; Paul named some of them in 1 Corinthians 6:9. In that day, idolatry and sensuality went together. "Effeminate" and "abusers" describe the passive and active partners in a homosexual relationship. (Paul dealt with this and with lesbianism in Romans 1:26–27.) In 1 Corinthians 6:10, Paul pointed his finger at the members guilty of sins of the spirit, those suing each other because of their covetous attitude.

But God can also cleanse sexual sins and make sinners into new creatures in Christ. "Ye are washed, but ye are sanctified, but ye are justified" (1 Cor. 6:11). The tenses of these verbs indicate a completed transaction. Now, because of all that God had done for them, they had an obligation to God to use their bodies for His service and His glory.

Consider God the Father (vv. 12–14). He created our bodies, and one day He will resurrect them in glory. (More about the resurrection in 1 Corinthians 15.) In view of the fact that our bodies have such a wonderful origin, and an even more wonderful future, how can we use them for such evil purposes?

The Corinthians had two arguments to defend their sensuality. First, "All things are lawful unto me" (1 Cor. 6:12). This was a popular phrase in Corinth, based on a false view of Christian freedom. We have not been set free so that we can enter into a new kind of bondage! As Christians, we must ask ourselves, "Will this enslave me? Is this activity really profitable for my spiritual life?"

Their second argument was, "Meats for the belly, and the belly for meats" (1 Cor. 6:13). They treated sex as an appetite to be satisfied and not as a gift to be cherished and used carefully. Sensuality is to sex what gluttony is to eating; both are sinful and both bring disastrous consequences. Just because we have certain normal desires, given by God at creation, does not mean that we must give in to them and always satisfy them. Sex outside of marriage is destructive, while sex in marriage can be creative and beautiful.

There may be excitement and enjoyment in sexual experience outside of marriage, *but there is not enrichment.* Sex outside of marriage is like a man robbing a bank: He gets something, but it is not his and he will one day pay for it. Sex within marriage can be like a person putting money into a bank: There is safety, security, and he will collect dividends. Sex within marriage can build a relationship that brings joys in the future; but sex apart from marriage has a way of weakening future relationships, as every Christian marriage counselor will tell you.

Consider God the Son (vv. 15–18). The believer's body is a member of Christ (1 Cor. 12:12ff.). How can we be joined to Christ and joined to sin at the same time? Such a thought astounds us. Yet some of the Corinthians saw no harm in visiting the temple prostitutes (there were a thousand of them at the temple of Aphrodite) and committing fornication.

Jesus Christ bought us with a price (1 Cor. 6:20), and therefore our bodies belong to Him. We are one spirit with the Lord, and we must yield our bodies to Him as living sacrifices (Rom. 12:1–2). If you begin each day by surrendering your body to Christ, it will make a great deal of difference in what you do with your body during the day.

Paul referred to the creation account (Gen. 2:24) to explain the seriousness of sexual sin. When a man and woman join their bodies, *the entire personality is involved.* There is a much deeper experience, a "oneness" that brings with it deep and lasting consequences. Paul warned that sexual sin is the most serious sin a person can commit against his body, for it involves the whole person (1 Cor. 6:18). Sex is not just a part of the body. Being "male" and "female" involves the total person. Therefore, sexual experience affects the total personality.

Paul did not suggest that being joined to a harlot was the equivalent of marriage, for marriage also involves *commitment.* The man and woman leave the parental home to begin a new home. This helps us to understand why sex *within marriage* can be an enriching experience of growth, because it is based on commitment. When two people pledge their love and faithfulness to each other, they lay a strong foundation on which to build. Marriage protects sex and enables the couple, committed to each other, to grow in this wonderful experience.

Consider God the Holy Spirit (vv. 19–20). God the Father created our bodies; God the Son redeemed them and made them part of His body; and God the Spirit indwells our bodies and makes them the very temple of God. How can we defile God's temple by using our bodies for immorality?

The word *your* is plural, but the words *body* and *temple* are singular (1 Cor. 6:19). It may be that Paul was here describing not only the individual believer, but also the local church. Each local assembly is a "body" of people united to Jesus Christ. The conduct of individual members affects the spiritual life of the entire church.

In both cases, the lesson is clear: "Glorify God in your body!" The Holy Spirit was given for the purpose of glorifying Jesus Christ (John 16:14). The Spirit can use our bodies to glorify Him and to magnify Him (Phil. 1:20–21). Our special relationship to the Holy Spirit brings with it a special responsibility.

So God the Father, God the Son, and God the Holy Spirit are all involved in what we do with our bodies. If we break God's laws, then we must pay the penalty (Rom. 1:24–27).

As you review this section, you will see that sexual sins affect the entire personality. They affect the *emotions,* leading to slavery (1 Cor. 6:12b). It is frightening to see how sensuality can get a hold of a person and defile his entire life, enslaving him to habits that destroy. It also affects a person *physically* (1 Cor. 6:18). The fornicator and adulterer, as well as the homosexual, may forget their sins, *but their sins will not forget them.*

In my pastoral counseling, I have had to help married couples whose relationship was falling apart because of the consequences of *pre*marital sex, as well as *extra*marital sex. The harvest of sowing to the flesh is sometimes delayed, but it is certain (Gal. 6:7–8). How sad it is to live with the consequences of *forgiven* sin.

Having said all this, we must also realize that there are *eternal* consequences for people who practice sexual sins. In 1 Corinthians 6:9–10, Paul *twice* stated that people who *practice* such sins will not inherit God's kingdom. A Christian may fall into these sins and be forgiven, as was David; but no Christian would *practice* such sins (1 John 3:1–10).

Finally, in all fairness, we must note that there are other sins besides sexual sins. For some reason, the church has often majored on condemning the sins of the Prodigal Son and has forgotten the sins of the elder brother (Luke 15:11–32). There are sins of the spirit as well as sins of the flesh— Paul names some of them in 1 Corinthians 6:10. Covetousness can send a man to hell just as easily as can adultery.

We must remember that the grace of God can change the sinner's life. "And such *were* some of you" (1 Cor. 6:11). It is wonderful how faith in Christ makes a sinner into a "new creation" (2 Cor. 5:17, 21). And it is important that we *live* like those who are a part of God's new creation. We are not our own. We belong to the Father who made us, the Son who redeemed us, and the Spirit who indwells us. We also belong to the people of God, the church, and our sins can weaken the testimony and infect the fellowship.

"Be ye holy; for I am holy" (1 Peter 1:16).

QUESTIONS FOR PERSONAL REFLECTION
OR GROUP DISCUSSION

1. When faced with a potential conflict with someone, are you more likely to fight? Flee? Ignore the problem and hope it goes away? Do something else?

2. Why do you think there was reluctance among the Corinthian church to deal with the sexual sin in their midst?

3. In what ways is church discipline similar to disciplining children? In what ways is it different?

4. What harm is there in not dealing with known sin?

5. Why was it important for the Corinthians to mourn over the sin (5:2)? To take action about the sin (5:3–5)?

6. Why should we not disassociate ourselves from sinners outside the church?

7. Why did Paul object to the Corinthian believers taking each other to court? Do you think Paul means that Christians should never take another Christian to court? Explain.

8. What was the Corinthians' rationale for sexual freedom? How does this rationalizing compare to modern-day attitudes toward sexuality?

9. Why is sexual immorality an offense to God the Father? God the Son? God the Spirit?

10. What hope do Christians have who have fallen into sin?

Chapter Six

BE WISE ABOUT CHRISTIAN MARRIAGE

(1 Corinthians 7)

U p to this point, Paul had been dealing with the sins reported to be known in the Corinthian congregation. Now he takes up the questions about which they had written to him: marriage (1 Cor. 7:1, 25), food offered to idols (1 Cor. 8:1), spiritual gifts (1 Cor. 12:1), the resurrection of the dead (1 Cor. 15:1), and the missionary offering for the Jews (1 Cor. 16:1).

As you study 1 Corinthians 7, please keep in mind that Paul is replying to definite questions. He is not spelling out a complete "theology of marriage" in one chapter. It is necessary to consider as well what the rest of the Bible has to say about this important subject.

Some liberal critics have accused Paul of being against both marriage and women. These accusations are not true, of course. Nor is it true that in 1 Corinthians 7:6, 10, 12, and 25 Paul was disclaiming divine inspiration for what he wrote. Rather, he was referring to what Jesus taught when He was on earth (Matt. 5:31–32; 19:1–12; Mark 10:1–12; Luke 16:18). Paul had to answer some questions that Jesus never discussed; but when a question arose that the Lord had dealt with, Paul referred to His words.

Instead of disclaiming inspiration, Paul claimed that what he wrote was equal in authority to what Christ taught.

Paul explained God's will concerning Christian marriage, and he addressed his counsel to three different groups of believers.

1. CHRISTIANS MARRIED TO CHRISTIANS (7:1–11)

Apparently one of the questions the church asked was, "Is celibacy [remaining unmarried] more spiritual than marriage?" Paul replied that it is good for a man or a woman to have the gift of celibacy, but the celibate state is not better than marriage, nor is it the best state for everybody. Dr. Kenneth Wuest translated Paul's reply, "It is perfectly proper, honorable, morally befitting for a man to live in strict celibacy."

First Corinthians 7:6 makes it clear that celibacy is permitted, but it is not commanded; and 1 Corinthians 7:7 informs us that not everybody has the gift of remaining celibate. This ties in with our Lord's teaching in Matthew 19:10–12, where "eunuchs" refers to those who abstain from marriage. "It is not good that the man should be alone" (Gen. 2:18) is generally true for most people; but some have been called to a life of singleness for one reason or another. Their singleness is not "subspiritual" or "superspiritual." It all depends on the will of God.

One purpose for marriage is "to avoid fornication." First Corinthians 7:2 makes it clear that God does not approve either of polygamy or homosexual "marriages." One man married to one woman has been God's pattern from the first. However, the husband and wife must not abuse the privilege of sexual love that is a normal part of marriage. The wife's body belongs to the husband, and the husband's body to the wife; and each must be considerate of the other. Sexual love is a beautiful tool to build with, not a weapon to fight with. To refuse each other is to commit robbery (1 Thess. 4:6) and to invite Satan to tempt the partners to seek their satisfaction elsewhere.

As in all things, the spiritual must govern the physical; for our bodies are God's temples. The husband and wife may abstain in order to devote their full interest to prayer and fasting (1 Cor. 7:5); but they must not use this as an excuse for prolonged separation. Paul is encouraging Christian partners to be "in tune" with each other in matters both spiritual and physical.

In 1 Corinthians 7:8–9, Paul applied the principle stated in 1 Corinthians 7:1 to single believers and widows: If you cannot control yourself, then marry.

Not only did the church ask about celibacy, but they also asked Paul about divorce. Since Jesus had dealt with this question, Paul cited His teaching: Husbands and wives are not to divorce each other (see also 1 Cor. 7:39). If divorce does occur, the parties should remain unmarried or seek reconciliation.

This is, of course, the ideal for marriage. Jesus did make one exception: If one party was guilty of fornication, this could be grounds for divorce. Far better that there be confession, forgiveness, and reconciliation; but if these are out of the question, then the innocent party may get a divorce. However, divorce is the last option; first, every means available should be used to restore the marriage.

It has been my experience as a pastor that when a husband and wife are yielded to the Lord, and when they seek to please each other in the marriage relationship, the marriage will be so satisfying that neither partner would think of looking elsewhere for fulfillment. "There are no sex problems in marriage," a Christian counselor once told me, "only personality problems with sex as one of the symptoms." The present frightening trend of increased divorces among Christians (and even among the clergy) must break the heart of God.

2. CHRISTIANS MARRIED TO NON-CHRISTIANS (7:12–24)

Some of the members of the Corinthian church were saved after they had been married, but their mates had not yet been converted. No doubt, some of these believers were having a difficult time at home; and they asked Paul, "Must we remain married to unsaved partners? Doesn't our conversion alter things?"

Paul replied that they were to remain with their unconverted mates so long as their mates were willing to live with them. Salvation does not alter the marriage state; if anything, it ought to enhance the marriage relationship. (Note Peter's counsel to wives with unsaved husbands in 1 Peter 3:1–6.) Since marriage is basically a physical relationship ("they shall be one flesh," Gen. 2:24), it can only be broken by a physical cause. Adultery and death would be two such causes (1 Cor. 7:39).

It is an act of disobedience for a Christian knowingly to marry an unsaved person (note "only in the Lord" in 1 Cor. 7:39; see also 2 Cor. 6:14). But if a person becomes a Christian after marriage, he should not use that as an excuse to break up the marriage just to avoid problems. In fact, Paul emphasized the fact that the Christian partner could have a spiritual influence on the unsaved mate. First Corinthians 7:14 does not teach that the unsaved partner is *saved* because of the believing mate, since each person must individually decide for Christ. Rather, it means that the believer exerts a spiritual influence in the home that can lead to the salvation of the lost partner.

What about the children? Again, the emphasis is on the influence of the godly partner. The believing husband or wife must not give up. In my own ministry, I have seen devoted Christians live for Christ in divided homes and eventually see their loved ones trust the Savior.

Salvation does not change the marriage state. If the wife's becoming a Christian annulled the marriage, then the children in the home would become illegitimate ("unclean" in 1 Cor. 7:14). Instead, these children may one day be saved if the Christian mate is faithful to the Lord.

It is difficult for us who are accustomed to the Christian faith to realize the impact that this new doctrine had on the Roman world. Here was a teaching for every person, regardless of race or social status. The church was perhaps the only assembly in the Roman Empire where slaves and freemen, men and women, rich and poor, could fellowship on an equal basis (Gal. 3:28). However, this new equality also brought with it some misunderstandings and problems; and some of these Paul dealt with in 1 Corinthians 7:17–24.

The principle that Paul laid down was this: Even though Christians are all one in Christ, each believer should remain in the same calling he was in when the Lord saved him. Jewish believers should not try to become Gentiles (by erasing the physical mark of the covenant), and Gentiles should not try to become Jews (by being circumcised). Slaves should not *demand* freedom from their Christian masters, just because of their equality in Christ. However, Paul *did* advise Christian slaves to secure their freedom if at all possible, probably by purchase. This same principle would apply to Christians married to unsaved mates.

But suppose the unsaved mate leaves the home? First Corinthians 7:15 gives the answer: The Christian partner is not obligated to keep the home together. We are called to peace, and we should do all we can to live in peace (Rom. 12:18); but there comes a time in some situations where peace is impossible. If the unsaved mate separates from his or her partner, there is little the Christian can do except to pray and continue to be faithful to the Lord.

Does separation then give the Christian mate the right to divorce and remarry? Paul did not say so. What if the unconverted mate ends up living with another partner? That would constitute adultery and give grounds for divorce. But even then, 1 Corinthians 7:10–11 would encourage forgiveness and restoration. Paul did not deal with every possible situation. He laid down spiritual principles, not a list of rules.

We are prone to think that a change in circumstances is always the answer to a problem. But the problem is usually *within* us and not *around* us. The heart of every problem is the problem in the heart. I have watched couples go through divorce and seek happiness in new circumstances, only to discover that they carried their problems with them. A Christian lawyer once told me, "About the only people who profit from divorces are the attorneys!"

3. UNMARRIED CHRISTIANS (7:25–40)

Paul had already addressed a brief word to this group in 1 Corinthians 7:8–9, but in this closing section of the chapter, he went into greater detail. Their question was, *"Must* a Christian get married? What about the unmarried women in the church who are not getting any younger?" (1 Cor. 7:36). Perhaps Paul addressed this section primarily to the parents of marriageable girls. Since Jesus did not give any special teaching on this topic, Paul gave his counsel as one taught of the Lord. He asked them to consider several factors when they made their decision about marriage.

First, consider the present circumstances (vv. 25–31). It was a time of distress (1 Cor. 7:26) when society was going through change (1 Cor. 7:31). There was not much time left for serving the Lord (1 Cor. 7:29). It is possible that there were political and economic pressures in Corinth about which we have no information. In view of the difficulties, it would be better for a person to be unmarried. However, this did not mean that married people should seek a divorce (1 Cor. 7:27). Paul's counsel was to the unmarried.

This did not mean that *nobody* should get married; but those who do marry must be ready to accept the trials that will accompany it (1 Cor. 7:28). In fact, the situation might become so difficult that even those already married will have to live as though they were not married (1 Cor. 7:29). Perhaps Paul was referring to husbands and wives being separated from each other because of economic distress or persecution.

To consider the circumstances is good counsel for engaged people today. The average age for first-time brides and grooms is climbing, which suggests that couples are waiting longer to get married. In my pastoral premarital counseling, I used to remind couples that the cheapest thing in a wedding was the marriage license. From then on, the prices would go up!

Second, face the responsibilities honestly (vv. 32–35). The emphasis in this paragraph is on the word *care,* which means "to be anxious, to be pulled in different directions." It is impossible for two people to live together without burdens of one kind or another, but there is no need to rush into marriage and create more problems. Marriage requires a measure of maturity, and age is no guarantee of maturity.

Once again, Paul emphasized living for the Lord. He did not suggest that it was impossible for a man or a woman to be married and serve God acceptably, because we know too many people who have done it. But the married servant of God must consider his or her mate, as well as the children God may give them; and this could lead to distraction. It is a fact of history that both John Wesley and George Whitefield might have been better off had they remained single—Wesley's wife finally left him, and Whitefield traveled so much that his wife was often alone for long periods of time.

It is possible to please both the Lord and your mate, if you are yielded to Christ and obeying the Word. Many of us have discovered that a happy home and satisfying marriage are a wonderful encouragement in the difficulties of Christian service. A well-known Scottish preacher was experiencing a great deal of public criticism because of a stand he took on a certain issue, and almost every day there was a negative report in the newspapers. A friend met him one day and asked, "How are you able to carry on in the face of this opposition?" The man replied quietly, "I am happy at home."

Unmarried believers who feel a call to serve God should examine their own hearts to see if marriage will help or hinder their ministry. They must also be careful to wed mates who feel a like call to serve God. Each person has his own gift and calling from God and must be obedient to His Word.

Third, each situation is unique (vv. 36–38). Paul addressed here the fathers of the unmarried girls. In that day, it was the parents who arranged the marriages, the father in particular (2 Cor. 11:2). Paul had already said in 1 Corinthians 7:35 that he was not laying down an ironclad rule for everybody to follow, regardless of circumstances. Now he made it clear that the father had freedom of choice whether or not he would give his daughter in marriage.

I have noticed that often in churches marriages come in "packs." One couple gets engaged and before long four couples are engaged. If all of these engagements are in the will of God, it can be a very exciting and wonderful experience; but I fear that some couples get engaged just to keep up with the crowd. Sometimes in Christian colleges, couples get what I call "senior panic" and rush out of engagement and into marriage immediately after graduation, lest they be left "waiting at the church." Sad to say, not all of these marriages are successful.

Even though our modern approach to dating and marriage was completely foreign to the Corinthians, the counsel Paul gave them still applies today. It is a wise thing for couples to counsel with their parents and with their Christian leaders in the church, lest they rush into something which afterward they regret.

Paul hit on a key problem in 1 Corinthians 7:36 when he mentioned "the flower of her age." This is a delicate phrase that simply means the girl is getting older. Dr. Kenneth Wuest translates it "past the bloom of her youth." She is starting to become one of the "unclaimed blessings" in the church. The danger, of course, is that she would rush into marriage just to avoid becoming a spinster, and she might make a mistake. A pastor friend of mine likes to say to couples, "Better to live in single loneliness than in married cussedness!"

Each situation is unique, and parents and children must seek the Lord's will. It takes more than two Christian people to make a happy marriage. Not every marriage that is scriptural is necessarily sensible.

Finally, remember that marriage is for life (vv. 39–40). It is God's will that the marriage union be permanent, a lifetime commitment. There is no place in Christian marriage for a "trial marriage," nor is there any room for the "escape hatch" attitude: "If the marriage doesn't work, we can always get a divorce."

For this reason, marriage must be built on something sturdier than good looks, money, romantic excitement, and social acceptance. There must be Christian commitment, character, and maturity. There must be a willingness to grow, to learn from each other, to forgive and forget, to minister to one another. The kind of love Paul described in 1 Corinthians 13 is what is needed to cement two lives together.

Paul closed the section by telling the widows that they were free to marry, but "only in the Lord" (1 Cor. 7:39). This means that they must not only marry believers, but marry in the will of God. Paul's counsel (for the reasons already given) was that they remain single, but he left the decision to them.

God has put "walls" around marriage, not to make it a prison, but to make it a safe fortress. The person who considers marriage a prison should not get married. When two people are lovingly and joyfully committed to each other—and to their Lord—the experience of marriage is one of enrichment and enlargement. They grow together and discover the richness of serving the Lord as a team in their home and church.

As you review this chapter, you cannot help but be impressed with the seriousness of marriage. Paul's counsel makes it clear that God takes marriage seriously, and that we cannot disobey God's Word without suffering painful consequences. While both Paul and Jesus leave room for divorce under certain conditions, this can never be God's first choice for a couple. God hates divorce (Mal. 2:14–16), and certainly no believer should consider divorce until all avenues of reconciliation have been patiently explored.

While a person's marital failure may hinder him from serving as a pastor or deacon (1 Tim. 3:2, 12), it need not keep him from ministering in other ways. Some of the best personal soul winners I have known have been men who, before their conversion, had the unfortunate experience of divorce. A man does not have to hold an office in order to have a ministry.

In summary, each person must ask himself or herself the following questions if marriage is being contemplated:

1. What is my gift from God?

2. Am I marrying a believer?

3. Are the circumstances such that marriage is right?

4. How will marriage affect my service for Christ?

5. Am I prepared to enter into this union for life?

QUESTIONS FOR PERSONAL REFLECTION
OR GROUP DISCUSSION

1. What did Paul advise for unmarried Christians?

2. What are the advantages of remaining single?

3. What did Paul have to say about separations and divorces in the church?

4. When, if ever, is divorce permitted by God? Support your understanding with Scripture.

5. In what cases, if any, is remarriage permitted after divorce?

6. If a person becomes a Christian after he has divorced and remarried, what should he do?

7. How can you defend the qualifier Paul used, "I, not the Lord" (1 Cor. 7:12), as being equally the authoritative Word of God?

8. How should we advise people with marital difficulties that are not specifically addressed in Scripture?

9. What do you think is God's reason for putting "walls" around marriage?

10. At the end of the chapter, Wiersbe lists some questions a person should consider before getting married. Which ones do you find especially helpful, and why?

Chapter Seven

BE WISE ABOUT CHRISTIAN LIBERTY

(1 Corinthians 8; 10)

After answering their questions about marriage, Paul turned to one of the most controversial subjects in the letter he received from the Corinthian church: "Can Christians eat meat that has been sacrificed to idols?" The immediate question does not interest believers today since we do not face that problem. But the wider issue of "Christian liberty" *does* apply to us, because we face questions that Paul never faced. Is it right for Christians to attend the theater? Should a believer have a television set in his home? To what extent can a Christian get involved in politics?

In 1 Corinthians 8—10, Paul enunciated four basic principles that would guide believers in making personal decisions about those "questionable" areas of the Christian life. The four principles are as follows:

Knowledge must be balanced by love (1 Cor. 8).

Authority must be balanced by discipline (1 Cor. 9).

Experience must be balanced by caution (1 Cor. 10:1–22).

Freedom must be balanced by responsibility (1 Cor. 10:23–33).

As you can see, Paul addressed himself primarily to the strong Christians in the church, believers who had spiritual knowledge and experience and who understood their authority and freedom in Christ. It is the strong who must care for the weak (Rom. 14—15).

The question of meats offered to idols is dealt with in 1 Corinthians 8; 10, so we will examine it in this chapter. In 1 Corinthians 9, Paul illustrated this principle of the right use of authority by explaining his own financial policy; so we will consider that in our next study.

KNOWLEDGE MUST BE BALANCED BY LOVE (8:1–13)

There were two sources of meat in the ancient world: the regular market (where the prices were higher) and the local temples (where meat from the sacrifices was always available). The strong members of the church realized that idols could not contaminate food, so they saved money by purchasing the cheaper meat available from the temples. Furthermore, if unconverted friends invited them to a feast at which sacrificial meat was served, the strong Christians attended it whether at the temple or in the home.

All of this offended the weaker Christians. Many of them had been saved out of pagan idolatry, and they could not understand why their fellow believers would want to have anything to do with meat sacrificed to idols. (In Romans 14—15, the weak Christians had problems over diets and holy days, but it was the same basic issue.) There was a potential division in the church, so the leaders asked Paul for counsel.

Paul called to their attention three important factors.

(1) **Knowledge (vv. 1–2).** The Corinthians were enriched in spiritual knowledge (1 Cor. 1:5) and were, in fact, rather proud of their achievements. They knew that an idol was nothing, merely the representation of a false god who existed only in the darkened minds of those who worshipped it. The presence of an idol in a temple was no solid proof that the god existed. (Later, Paul would point out that idolatry was basically the worship of

demons.) So the conclusion was logical: A nonexistent god could not contaminate food offered on his altar.

So far, it is the strong Christians who are ahead. Why, then, are the weak Christians upset with them, when their position is so logical? Because you don't always solve every problem with logic. The little child who is afraid of the dark will not be assured by arguments, especially if the adult (or older brother) adopts a superior attitude. Knowledge can be a weapon to fight with or a tool to build with, depending on how it is used. If it "puffs up" then it cannot "build up [edify]."

A know-it-all attitude is only an evidence of ignorance. The person who really knows truth is only too conscious of how much he does not know. Furthermore, it is one thing to know *doctrine* and quite something else to know *God*. It is possible to grow in Bible knowledge and yet not grow in grace or in one's personal relationship with God. The test is *love,* which is the second factor Paul discussed.

(2) Love (vv. 3–6). Love and knowledge must go together, "speaking the truth in love" (Eph. 4:15). It has well been said, "Truth without love is brutality, but love without truth is hypocrisy." Knowledge is power and it must be used in love. But love must always be controlled by knowledge (see Paul's prayer in Phil. 1:9–11). The strong believers in the church had knowledge, but they were not using their knowledge in love. Instead of building up the weak saints, the strong Christians were only puffing up themselves.

Paul's great concern was that the strong saints help the weaker saints to grow and to stop being weak saints. Some people have the false notion that the *strong* Christians are the ones who live by rules and regulations and who get offended when others exercise their freedom in Christ; but such is not the case. It is the *weak* Christians who must have the security of law and who are afraid to use their freedom in Christ. It is the weak Christians who are prone to judge and criticize stronger believers and to stumble over what they do. This, of course, makes it difficult for the strong saints to minister to their weaker brothers and sisters.

It is here that love enters the picture, for "love builds up" and puts others first. When spiritual knowledge is used in love, the stronger Christian can take the hand of the weaker Christian and help him to stand and walk so as to enjoy his freedom in Christ. *You cannot force-feed immature believers and transform them into giants.* Knowledge must be mixed with love; otherwise, the saints will end up with "big heads" instead of enlarged hearts. A famous preacher used to say, "Some Christians grow; others just swell."

Knowledge and love are two important factors, for knowledge must be balanced by love if we are to use our Christian freedom in the right way. But there is a third factor.

(3) Conscience (vv. 7–13). The word *conscience* simply means "to know with," and it is used thirty-two times in the New Testament. Conscience is that internal court where our actions are judged and are either approved or condemned (Rom. 2:14–15). Conscience is not the law; it bears witness to God's moral law. But the important thing is this: *Conscience depends on knowledge.* The more spiritual knowledge we know and *act on,* the stronger the conscience will become.

Some Christians have weak consciences because they have been saved only a short time and have not had opportunity to grow. Like little babes in the home, they must be guarded carefully. Other saints have weak consciences because they *will not* grow. They ignore their Bibles and Christian fellowship and remain in a state of infancy (1 Cor. 3:1–4; Heb. 5:11–14). But some believers remain weak because they are afraid of freedom. They are like a child old enough to go to school, who is afraid to leave home and must be taken to school each day.

The conscience of a weak Christian is easily defiled (1 Cor. 8:7), wounded (1 Cor. 8:12), and offended (1 Cor. 8:13). For this reason, the stronger saints must defer to the weaker saints and do nothing that would harm them. It might not harm the mature saint to share a feast in an idolatrous temple, but it might harm his weaker brother. First Corinthians 8:10 warns that the immature believer might decide to imitate his stronger brother and thus be led into sin.

It is important to note that the stronger believer defers to the weaker believer in love *only that he might help him to mature.* He does not "pamper" him; he seeks to edify him, to help him grow. Otherwise, *both* will become weak.

We are free in Christ, but we must take care that our spiritual knowledge is tempered by love, and that we do not tempt the weaker Christian to run ahead of his conscience. Where knowledge is balanced by love, the strong Christian will have a ministry to the weak Christian, and the weak Christian will grow and become strong.

EXPERIENCE MUST BE BALANCED BY CAUTION (10:1–22)

Paul reminded the experienced believers who were strong in the faith that they had better not grow overconfident in their ability to overcome temptation. "Wherefore let him that thinketh he standeth take heed lest he fall" (1 Cor. 10:12). Paul used the nation of Israel as his example to warn the mature believers that their experience must be balanced by caution. He gave three warnings.

First, he warned that privileges were no guarantee of success (vv. 1–4). Israel had been delivered from Egypt by the power of God, just as the Christian believer has been redeemed from sin. (In 1 Corinthians 5:7–8, Paul had already related Passover to salvation.) Israel was identified with Moses in their Red Sea "baptism," just as the Corinthians had been identified with Christ in their Christian baptism. Israel ate the manna from heaven and drank the water God provided, just as Christians nourish themselves on the spiritual sustenance God supplies (John 6:63, 68; 7:37–39). However, these spiritual privileges did not prevent the Jews from falling into sin.

There are dangers to maturity as well as to immaturity, and one of them is overconfidence. When we think we are strong, we discover that we are weak. The strong believer who eats in the temple may find himself struggling with an enemy who is too strong for him.

Paul did not suggest in 1 Corinthians 10:4 that an actual rock accompanied the Jews throughout their wilderness journey, though some Jewish rabbis taught this idea. It was a *spiritual* rock that supplied what they needed, and that Rock was Christ. Sometimes the water came from a rock (Ex. 17:1–7; Num. 20:7–11) and at other times from a well (Num. 21:16–18). God provided the water.

Paul issued a second warning: Good beginnings do not guarantee good endings (vv. 5–12). The Jews experienced God's miracles, and yet they failed when they were tested in the wilderness. Experience must always be balanced with caution, for we never come to the place in our Christian walk where we are free from temptation and potential failure. All of the Jews twenty years old and upward who were rescued from Egypt, except for Joshua and Caleb, died in the wilderness during their years of wandering (Num. 14:26ff.).

We can hear some of the "strong" Corinthians asking, "But what does that have to do with us?" Paul then pointed out that the Corinthian church was guilty of the same sins that the Jews committed. Because of their lust for evil things, the Corinthians were guilty of immorality (1 Cor. 6), idolatry (1 Cor. 8; 10), and murmuring against God (2 Cor. 12:20–21). Like the nation of Israel, they were tempting God and just "daring Him" to act.

Paul certainly knew his Old Testament, and his readers would recognize the events referred to. The "lusting" is found in Numbers 11:4ff., the idolatry in Exodus 32, and the fornication in Numbers 25. The Israelites often tempted God, but perhaps Numbers 21:4–6 was the reference Paul had in mind. For their complaining, see Numbers 14 and 16.

This kind of sin is serious and God must judge it. Not only did some of these rebels immediately die (1 Cor. 11:29–31), but those who remained were not permitted to enter the Promised Land. They were saved from Egypt but were not privileged to claim their rich inheritance. Paul was not suggesting that his readers might lose their salvation, but he was afraid that some of them would be "castaways" (1 Cor. 9:27), disapproved of God and unable to receive any reward.

I heard about a pastor who gave a series of sermons on "The Sins of the Saints." One member of the church, apparently under conviction, disapproved of the series and told the pastor so. "After all," she said, "sin in the life of a Christian is different from sin in the life of an unsaved person."

"Yes, it is," the pastor replied. "It's *worse!*"

We must not think that because the Jews were under the law that their sins were worse than ours and therefore dealt with more severely. Sin in the church today is far more serious, because we have Israel's example to learn from, and we are living "at the end of the ages." To sin against the law is one thing; to sin against grace is quite something else.

Paul's third warning was that God can enable us to overcome temptation if we heed His Word (vv. 13–22). God permits us to be tempted because He knows how much we can take; and He always provides a way to escape if we will trust Him and take advantage of it. The believer who thinks he can stand may fall; but the believer who flees will be able to stand.

Paul had already told his readers to "flee fornication" (1 Cor. 6:18); and now his warning is "Flee from idolatry" (1 Cor. 10:14). He explained the reason why: The idol itself is nothing, but it can be used by Satan to lead you into sin. Idolatry is demonic (Deut. 32:17; Ps. 106:37). To sit at an idol's table could mean fellowship ("communion, partakers") with demons. Paul was again enforcing the important doctrine of separation from sin (2 Cor. 6:1—7:1).

He used the Lord's Supper as an illustration. When the believer partakes of the cup and loaf at the Lord's Table, he is, in a spiritual way, having fellowship with the body and blood of Christ. By remembering Christ's death, the believer enters into a communion with the risen Lord. In 1 Corinthians 10:18, Paul pointed to the temple altar and sacrifices as another illustration of this truth. The application is clear: A believer cannot partake of the Lord's food (the Old Testament sacrifice, the New Testament supper) and the Devil's food (the idol's table) without exposing himself to danger and provoking the Lord.

"Are we stronger than he?" (1 Cor. 10:22) is directed at the strong Christian who was sure he could enjoy his liberty in the pagan temple and not be harmed. "You may be stronger than your weaker brother," Paul intimated, "but you are not stronger than God!" It is dangerous to play with sin and tempt God.

FREEDOM MUST BE BALANCED BY RESPONSIBILITY (10:23–33)

At no time did Paul deny the freedom of the mature Christian to enjoy his privileges in Christ. "All things are lawful"—*but* not everything is profitable, and some things lead to slavery (1 Cor. 6:12). "All things are profitable"—*but* some activities can cause your weaker brother to stumble (1 Cor. 8:11–13). In other words, it is a mark of maturity when we balance our freedom with responsibility; otherwise, it ceases to be freedom and becomes anarchy, lawlessness.

To begin with, we have a responsibility to our fellow Christians in the church (1 Cor. 10:23–30). We are responsible to build others up in the faith and to seek their advantage. Philippians 2:1–4 gives the same admonition. While we do have freedom in Christ, we are not free to harm another believer.

Paul applied this truth to the impending question of meat offered to idols. He had already warned against a believer *publicly* participating in pagan feasts (1 Cor. 8:9–13), so now he dealt with *private* meals. In

1 Corinthians 10:25–26, he instructed the believers to ask no questions about the meat purchased at the market for use in their own homes. After all, everything comes from God (he quoted Ps. 24:1), and all food is permissible to the believer (Mark 7:14–23; Acts 10:9–16, 28; 1 Tim. 4:3–5). The mature believer can enjoy in his own home even meat sacrificed to idols. Even if meat purchased at the regular market originally came from the temple (which was often the case), he would not be harmed.

But what about those times when the believer is the guest in the home of an unbeliever? Paul handled that problem in 1 Corinthians 10:27–30. If the Christian feels disposed to go (Paul did not make this decision a matter of great import), he should eat whatever is set before him and ask no questions (Luke 10:8; 1 Tim. 6:17). However, there may be present at the meal one of the weaker brothers or sisters who wants to avoid meat offered to idols and who has done some investigating. If this weaker saint informs the stronger Christian that the meat indeed has been offered to idols, then the stronger saint must not eat it. If he did, he would cause the weaker believer to stumble and possibly to sin.

Paul anticipated the objections. "Why should I not enjoy food for which I give thanks? Why should my liberty be curtailed because of another person's weak conscience?" His reply introduced the second responsibility we have: *We are responsible to glorify God in all things* (1 Cor. 10:31). We cannot glorify God by causing another Christian to stumble. To be sure, our own conscience may be strong enough for us to participate in some activity and not be harmed. But we dare not use our freedom in Christ in any way that will injure a fellow Christian.

But there is a third responsibility that ties in with the first two: *We are responsible to seek to win the lost* (1 Cor. 10:32–33). We must not make it difficult either for Jews or Gentiles to trust the Lord, or for other members of the church to witness for the Lord. We must not live to seek our own benefit ("profit"), but also the benefit of others, that they might be saved.

When Paul wrote, "I please all men in all things" (1 Cor. 10:33), he was not suggesting that he was a compromiser or a man-pleaser (Gal. 1:10). He was affirming the fact that his life and ministry were centered on helping others rather than on promoting himself and his own desires.

Before we leave this important section, we ought to note the fact that Paul probably appeared inconsistent to those who did not understand his principles of Christian living. At times, he would eat what the Gentiles were eating. At other times, he would eat only "kosher" food with the Jews. But instead of being inconsistent, he was actually living *consistently* by the principles he laid down in these chapters. A weather vane seems inconsistent, first pointing in one direction and then in another. But a weather vane is always consistent: It always points toward the direction where the wind is blowing. That is what makes it useful.

Are there some things that a mature Christian can do in the privacy of his own home that he would not do in public? Yes, provided they do not harm him personally and he does not tempt the Lord. I know a couple who, when their children were small, eliminated all games from their home that used either cards or dice. When their children were more mature, they were permitted to play those games.

As Christians, we *do* have freedom. This freedom was purchased for us by Jesus Christ, so it is very precious. Freedom comes from knowledge: "And ye shall know the truth, and the truth shall make you free" (John 8:32). The more we understand about the atom, for example, the more freedom we have to use it wisely. However, knowledge must be balanced by love; otherwise, it will tear down instead of build up.

The strong Christian not only has knowledge, but he also has experience. He can look back and see how the Lord has dealt with him through the years. But he must be careful, for experience must be balanced with caution. Take heed, lest you fall!

The strong Christian knows that he has this freedom, but he also knows that freedom involves responsibility. I have the freedom, for example, to take my car out of the garage and drive it on the highway; *but I must drive it responsibly.* I am not free to drive at any speed on my street; nor am I free to ignore the traffic signs along the way.

Out of these chapters come several "tests" we may apply to our own decisions and activities.

"All things are lawful," *but—*

1. Will they lead to freedom or slavery? (1 Cor. 6:12)

2. Will they make me a stumbling block or a stepping-stone?
   (1 Cor. 8:13)

3. Will they build me up or tear me down?
   (1 Cor. 10:23)

4. Will they only please me, or will they glorify Christ?
   (1 Cor. 10:31)

5. Will they help to win the lost to Christ or turn them away?
   (1 Cor. 10:33)

The way we use our freedom and relate to others indicates whether we are mature in Christ. Strong and weak Christians need to work together in love to edify one another and glorify Jesus Christ.

QUESTIONS FOR PERSONAL REFLECTION
OR GROUP DISCUSSION

1. What are some ethical issues that might be considered debatable among Christians today? (For example, the Bible says nothing directly about the use of television.)

2. What did Paul mean by "strong" Christians? By "weak" Christians?

3. Why is there often friction between weaker and stronger Christians? Who should take responsibility for solving these conflicts? Why?

4. Why did the Corinthians need to balance knowledge with love?

5. For what purpose should the stronger Christian sometimes defer to the weaker? Are there any circumstances in which the stronger Christian should not defer to the weaker?

6. To what does overconfidence in our ability to resist temptation lead? Why?

7. What do you make of the fact that Paul lists the sin of grumbling against God (10:10) alongside idolatry and sexual immorality?

8. What lessons can we learn from the failure of the Israelites and the Corinthians?

9. In light of what Paul says in these chapters, could a strong Christian attend a séance with the goal of winning to Christ those who are involved in the occult? What would be the arguments for or against doing so? (Consider Wiersbe's closing list of questions.)

10. What are some principles in these chapters that will help you make decisions about gray areas?

Chapter Eight

Be Wise about Personal Priorities

(1 Corinthians 9)

This chapter deals with Paul's policy of financial support, and it appears to be an interruption of his discussion of "meats offered to idols." Actually, it is not an interruption; it is an illustration of the very principles that he presents in 1 Corinthians 8 and 10. Paul used himself as an illustration of the mature use of liberty: He was free to receive financial support from the Corinthian church, yet he set aside that right in order to achieve a higher goal.

Keep in mind that, for the most part, the Greeks despised manual labor. They had slaves to do manual labor so that the citizens could enjoy sports, philosophy, and leisure. The Jews, of course, magnified honest labor. Even the learned rabbis each practiced a trade, and they taught the people, "He who does not teach his son to work, teaches him to be a thief." Paul was trained as a tentmaker, a worker in leather.

In order to illustrate the Christian use of personal rights, Paul presented a twofold defense of his financial policy as a servant of Christ.

1. HE DEFENDED HIS RIGHT TO RECEIVE SUPPORT (9:1–14)

In this first half of the chapter, Paul proved that he had the right to receive financial support from the church at Corinth. He gave five arguments to support this contention.

(1) His apostleship (vv. 1–6). The word *apostle* means "one sent under commission" and refers primarily to the twelve apostles and Paul. These men had a special commission, along with the New Testament prophets, to lay the foundation of the church (Eph. 2:20). One of the qualifications for being an apostle was a personal experience of seeing the resurrected Christ (Acts 1:21–22). Paul saw the Lord when he was traveling to Damascus to arrest Christians (Acts 9:1–9). The apostles were to be witnesses of Christ's resurrection (Acts 2:32; 3:15; 5:32; 10:39–43).

The apostles also were given the ability to perform special signs and wonders to attest the message that they preached (Heb. 2:4). Paul had performed such miracles during his ministry in Corinth (2 Cor. 12:12). In fact, Paul considered the Corinthian church a very special "seal" of his ministry as an apostle. Corinth was a difficult city to minister in, and yet Paul accomplished a great work because of the Lord's enablement (see Acts 18:1–17).

Therefore, as an apostle, Paul had the right to receive support from the people to whom he ministered. (The word *power* is used six times in this chapter, and means "authority, right.") The apostle was the representative of Christ; he deserved to be welcomed and cared for. Paul was unmarried; but if he'd had a wife, she, too, would have had the right to be supported by the church. Peter was a married man (Mark 1:30), and his wife traveled with him. Paul had the same right, but he did not use it.

Paul also had the right to devote his full time to the ministry of the Word. He did not have to make tents. The other apostles did not work to support themselves because they gave themselves completely to the ministry of the Word. However, both Paul and Barnabas labored with their own hands to support not only themselves, but also the men who labored with them.

(2) Human experience (v. 7). Everyday experience teaches us that a workman deserves some reward for his labors. If a man is drafted to be a soldier, the government pays his wages and provides a certain amount of supplies for him. The man who plants a vineyard gets to eat the fruit, just as the shepherd or herdsman has the right to use the milk from the animals.

Perhaps in the back of his mind, Paul was comparing the church to an army, a vineyard, and a flock. As an apostle, Paul was in the very front line of the battle. He had already compared the church at Corinth to a cultivated field (1 Cor. 3:6–9), and the Lord Himself had used the image of the vine and branches (John 15) as well as the flock (John 10). The lesson was clear: The Christian worker has the right to expect benefits for his labors. If this is true in the "secular" realm, it is also true in the spiritual realm.

(3) The Old Testament law (vv. 8–12). The Old Testament was the "Bible" of the early church, since the New Testament was in the process of being written. The first believers found guidance in the spiritual principles of the law, even though they had been liberated from obeying the commandments of the law. Saint Augustine said, "The New is in the Old concealed; the Old is by the New revealed."

Paul quoted Deuteronomy 25:4 to prove his point. (He quoted this same verse when he wrote to Timothy and encouraged the church to pay their ministers adequately, 1 Tim. 5:17–18.) Since oxen cannot read, this verse was not written for them. Nor was it written only for the farmer who was using the labors of the ox. It would be cruel for the farmer to bind the mouth of the ox and prevent him from eating the available grain. After all, the ox was doing the work.

Paul correctly saw a spiritual principle in this commandment: The laborer has the right to share in the bounties. The ox had plowed the soil in preparation for sowing, and now he was treading out the grain that had been harvested. Paul had plowed the soil in Corinth. He had seen a harvest from the seed he had planted. It was only right that he enjoyed some of the fruits of that harvest.

First Corinthians 9:11 enunciates a basic principle of the Christian life: If we receive *spiritual* blessings, we should in turn share *material* blessings. For example, the Jews gave spiritual blessings to the Gentiles; so the Gentiles had an obligation to share materially with the Jews (Rom. 15:25–27). Those who teach us the Word have the right to expect us to support them (Gal. 6:6–10).

We have reason to believe that Paul did accept financial support from other churches. The Philippian believers sent him two gifts when he went to Thessalonica (Phil. 4:15–16). "I robbed other churches, taking wages of them, to do you service," Paul reminded the Corinthians (2 Cor. 11:8). Apparently other ministers had accepted support at Corinth (1 Cor. 9:12), but Paul preferred to remain independent "lest we should hinder the gospel of Christ." He wanted to be the best example possible to other believers (2 Thess. 3:6–9).

(4) Old Testament practice (v. 13). The priests and Levites lived off of the sacrifices and offerings that were brought to the temple. The regulations governing their part of the offerings, and the special tithes they received, also are found in Numbers 18:8–32; Leviticus 6:14—7:36; and 27:6–33. The application is clear: If the Old Testament ministers under law were supported by the people to whom they ministered, should not God's servants who minister under grace also be supported?

(5) The teaching of Jesus (v. 14). Paul was no doubt referring to our Lord's words recorded in Luke 10:7–8 and Matthew 10:10. The Corinthians did not have a copy of either gospel to refer to, but the Lord's teaching would have been given to them as a part of the oral tradition shared by the apostles. *The laborer is worthy of his hire* is a fundamental principle that the church dare not neglect.

Paul certainly proved his point. His five arguments proved conclusively that he had the right to expect the Corinthian believers to support him in his ministry when he was with them. Yet he had deliberately refused their support. Why? This he explained in the second part of his defense.

2. HE DEFENDED HIS RIGHT TO REFUSE SUPPORT (9:15–27)

Paul had the authority (right) to receive material support, but being a mature Christian, he balanced his authority with discipline. He did not have the right to give up his liberty in Christ, but he did have the liberty to give up his rights. Now we understand why he wrote as he did: He gave the Corinthian believers a living example of the very principles he was writing about. Should not the stronger believers in the church be able to set aside their rights for the sake of the weaker saints? Was eating meat more important than edifying the church?

Paul was talking about *priorities,* the things that are really important to us in our lives. It is unfortunate that some Christians have their personal priorities confused and, as a result, are hindering the work of Christ. If each believer were practicing Matthew 6:33, there would be plenty of money for missions, plenty of manpower for service, and the work of the Lord would prosper. But not every Christian is practicing Matthew 6:33.

A woman sent a gift to a ministry and explained that it was money she had saved because she had turned off the hot water tank in her house. She also did without a daily paper so that she might have more to give to the Lord's work. When she took a bath, she heated the water on the stove, "just the way we did it when we were kids." The Lord may not call all of us to this kind of sacrifice, but her example is worthy of respect.

Paul gave three reasons that explained why he had refused support from the Corinthian church.

(1) For the gospel's sake (vv. 15–18). Paul did not want to "hinder the gospel of Christ" (1 Cor. 9:12). In that day, the Greek cities were filled with all kinds of itinerant teachers and preachers, most of whom were out to make money. Not only had Paul refused to use the kind of oratory and arguments that these teachers used (1 Cor. 2:1–5), but he also refused to accept money from those to whom he ministered. He wanted the message of the gospel to be free from any obstacles or hindrances in the minds of lost sinners.

For that matter, when Paul added "neither have I written these things" (1 Cor. 9:15), he was making sure that his readers did not get the idea that he was "hinting" that they should support him!

Paul could not claim any credit for preaching the gospel, because he had been called of God to preach. "Necessity is laid upon me; yea, woe is unto me, if I preach not the gospel!" (1 Cor. 9:16). God had given him a divine stewardship ("dispensation"), and "it is required in stewards, that a man be found faithful" (1 Cor. 4:2). God would see to it that Paul would receive his wages (*reward*—same word translated "hire" in Luke 10:7).

What was Paul's reward? The joy of preaching the gospel without charge! This meant that no man could accuse him of underhanded motives or methods as he shared the good news of Jesus Christ.

It is unfortunate when the ministry of the gospel is sometimes hindered by an overemphasis on money. The unsaved world is convinced that most preachers and missionaries are only involved in "religious rackets" to take money from innocent people. No doubt there are religious racketeers in the world today (1 Tim. 6:3–16), people who use religion to exploit others and control them. We would certainly not agree with their purposes or their practices. We must make sure that nothing we do in our own ministry gives the impression that we are of their number.

A wrong attitude toward money has hindered the gospel from the earliest days of the church. Ananias and Sapphira loved money more than they loved the truth, and God killed them (Acts 5). Simon the magician thought he could buy the gift of the Spirit with money (Acts 8:18–24). His name is now in the dictionary. *Simony* is the practice of buying and selling religious offices and privileges.

For eighteen fruitful years, Dr. H. A. Ironside pastored the Moody Church in Chicago. I recall the first time I heard him announce an offering. He said, "We ask God's people to give generously. If you are not a believer in Jesus Christ, we do not ask you to give. We have a gift for you—eternal life through faith in Christ!" He made it clear that the offering was for believers, lest the unsaved in the congregation stumble over money and then reject the gospel.

(2) For the sinners' sake (vv. 19–23). What a paradox: free from all men, yet the servant of all men! "Ourselves your servants for Jesus' sake" (2 Cor. 4:5). Because he was free, Paul was able to serve others and to set aside his own rights for their sake.

It is unfortunate that the phrase "all things to all men" (1 Cor. 9:22) has been used and abused by the world and made to mean what Paul did not intend for it to mean. Paul was not a chameleon who changed his message and methods with each new situation. Nor was Paul a compromiser who adjusted his message to please his audience. He was an ambassador, not a politician!

Paul was a Jew who had a great burden for his own people (Rom. 9:1–3; 10:1). But his special calling was to minister to the Gentiles (Eph. 3:8). Whenever he went into a new city (and he always went where the gospel had not yet been preached, Rom. 15:20), he headed straight for the synagogue, if there was one, and boldly shared the gospel. If he was rejected by the Jews, then he turned to the Gentiles.

What separated Jews and Gentiles in that day? The law and the covenants (Eph. 2:11–15). In his personal life, Paul so lived that he did not offend either the Jews or the Gentiles. He did not parade his liberty before the Jews, nor did he impose the law on the Gentiles.

Was Paul behaving in an inconsistent manner? Of course not. He simply adapted his approach to different groups. When you read his sermons in the book of Acts, you see this wise adaptation. When he preached to Jews, he started with the Old Testament patriarchs; but when he preached to Gentiles, he began with the God of creation. Paul did not have a "stock sermon" for all occasions.

It is worth noting that our Lord followed the same approach. To the highborn Jew, Nicodemus, He talked about spiritual birth (John 3); but to the Samaritan woman, He spoke about living water (John 4). Jesus was flexible and adaptable, and Paul followed His example. Neither Jesus nor Paul had an inflexible "evangelistic formula" that was used in every situation.

It takes tact to have contact. When the people I witness to tell me about their experience of confirmation, I tell them that I, too, was confirmed. I express my appreciation for the pastor who taught me and prayed for me. Then I tell them, "A year after I was confirmed, I met Jesus Christ personally and was born again." A good witness tries to build bridges, not walls.

To immature people, Paul's lifestyle probably looked inconsistent. In reality, he was very consistent, for his overriding purpose was to win people to Jesus Christ. Consistency can become a very legalistic thing, and a man can become so bound by man-made rules and standards that he has no freedom to minister. He is like young David trying to battle in Saul's armor.

Paul had the right to eat whatever pleased him, but he gave up that right so that he might win the Jews. Paul revered the law (Rom. 7:12), but set that aside so that he might reach the lost Gentiles. He even identified himself with the legalistic weak Christians so that he might help them to grow. It was not compromise, but rather total abandonment to the higher law of love. Paul followed the example of the Savior and humbled himself to become the servant of all.

(3) For his own sake (vv. 24–27). Paul was fond of athletic images and used them often in his letters. The Corinthians would have been familiar with the Greek Olympic Games as well as their own local Isthmian Games. Knowing this, Paul used a metaphor very close to their experience.

An athlete must be disciplined if he is to win the prize. Discipline means giving up the good and the better for the best. The athlete must watch his diet as well as his hours. He must smile and say, "No, thank you," when people offer him fattening desserts or invite him to late-night parties. There is nothing wrong with food or fun, but if they interfere with your highest goals, then they are hindrances and not helps.

The Christian does not run the race in order to get to heaven. He is in the race because he has been saved through faith in Jesus Christ. Only Greek citizens were allowed to participate in the games, and they had to obey the rules both in their training and in their performing. Any contestant found breaking the training rules was automatically disqualified.

In order to give up his rights and have the joy of winning lost souls, Paul had to discipline himself. That is the emphasis of this entire chapter: Authority (rights) must be balanced by discipline. If we want to serve the Lord and win His reward and approval, we must pay the price.

The word *castaway* (1 Cor. 9:27) is a technical word familiar to those who knew the Greek games. It means "disapproved, disqualified." At the Greek games, there was a herald who announced the rules of the contest, the names of the contestants, and the names and cities of the winners. He would also announce the names of any contestants who were disqualified.

Paul saw himself as both a "herald" and a "runner." He was concerned lest he get so busy trying to help others in the race that he ignore himself and find himself disqualified. Again, it was not a matter of losing personal salvation. (The disqualified Greek athlete did not lose his citizenship, only his opportunity to win a prize.) The whole emphasis is on *rewards*, and Paul did not want to lose his reward.

Only one runner could win the olive-wreath crown in the Greek games, but *every* believer can win an incorruptible crown when he stands before the judgment seat of Christ. This crown is given to those who discipline themselves for the sake of serving Christ and winning lost souls. They keep their bodies under control and keep their eyes on the goal.

In recent years, evangelical Christians have rediscovered the importance of personal discipline and the relationship between a disciplined body and a Spirit-filled life. We must, of course, avoid extremes. On the one hand, religious asceticism is unhealthy and of no value spiritually (Col. 2:18–23). But on the other hand, there is something to be said for disciplined eating, exercising, and resting, and a Spirit-directed balanced life. We smugly congratulate ourselves that we do not smoke or use alcohol, but what about our overeating and obesity? And many Christians cannot discipline their time so as to have a consistent devotional life or Bible-study program.

Paul had one great goal in life: to glorify the Lord by winning the lost and building up the saints. To reach this goal, he was willing to pay any price. *He was willing even to give up his personal rights!* He sacrificed immediate gains for eternal rewards, immediate pleasures for eternal joys.

QUESTIONS FOR PERSONAL REFLECTION
OR GROUP DISCUSSION

1. What rights do we have as humans? What happens when someone violates one of your rights?

2. What is Paul's defense of his financial policy?

3. What special relationship does Paul have with the Corinthians?

4. In 1 Corinthians 9:19, Paul states that he is free but also a slave. What does he mean?

5. What does Paul mean when he says he is all things to all people? How is this different from being a people pleaser in a negative sense?

6. What are appropriate ways for you to accommodate yourself to unbelievers for the sake of the gospel?

7. What is the connection between 1 Corinthians 9 and Paul's discussion about meat offered to idols in 1 Corinthians 8?

8. What rights do you have that God may want you to give up?

9. What is the "race" Paul talks about, and how should a believer prepare for this race?

10. What might be considered encumbrances that hinder you from running your best race? What should you do about these?

Chapter Nine

BE WISE ABOUT CHURCH ORDER

(1 Corinthians 11)

S ince Paul had some negative things to say to the church later in this section, he opened it on a positive note by praising the church. Two matters in particular merited praise: The church remembered Paul and appreciated him, and the church was faithful to keep the teaching that had been given them. The word *ordinances* simply means "traditions," teachings that were passed on from one person to another (2 Tim. 2:2). The traditions of men should be avoided (Matt. 15:2–3; Col. 2:8), but the traditions that are given in the Word of God must be observed.

One of the biggest problems in the Corinthian church was disorder in the public meetings. Some of the women were assuming more freedom than they should have; there was disorder at the Lord's Supper; and there was confusion in the use of the spiritual gifts. The church had been greatly enriched with spiritual *gifts,* but they were sadly lacking in spiritual *graces.*

Paul could have tried to solve these problems by issuing apostolic edicts, but instead he patiently explained the spiritual principles that supported the teachings he had given the church. He founded his arguments on the Word of God.

Paul dealt with three particular areas of confusion in their public worship.

1. WOMEN PRAYING AND PROPHESYING (11:3–16)

The Christian faith brought freedom and hope to women, children, and slaves. It taught that all people, regardless of race or sex, were equal before their Creator, and that all believers were one in Jesus Christ (Gal. 3:28). As we have noted before, the local church was perhaps the only fellowship in the Roman Empire that welcomed all people, regardless of nationality, social status, sex, or economic position.

It was to be expected that there would be some who would carry this newfound freedom to excess. A new movement always suffers more from its disciples than from its enemies, and this was true in Corinth. Some of the women flaunted their "freedom" in the public meetings by refusing to cover their heads when they participated.

Paul did not forbid the women to pray or to prophesy. (Prophesying is not quite the same as our "preaching" or "expounding the Word." A person with the gift of prophecy proclaimed God's message as it was given to him *immediately* by the Spirit. The modern preacher studies the Word and prepares his message.) While the New Testament does not seem to permit women elders (1 Tim. 3:2), women in the early church who had the gift of prophecy were allowed to exercise it. They were also permitted to pray in the public meetings. However, they were not permitted to usurp authority over the men (1 Tim. 2:11–15) or to judge the messages of the other prophets (1 Cor. 14:27–35). If they had any questions, they were to ask their husbands (or other men) outside of the church meeting.

Eastern society at that time was very jealous over its women. Except for the temple prostitutes, the women wore long hair and, in public, wore a covering over their heads. (Paul did not use the word *veil*, i.e., a covering over the face. The woman put the regular shawl over her head, and this covering symbolized her submission and purity.) For the Christian women in the church to appear in public without the covering, let alone to pray and share the Word, was both daring and blasphemous.

Paul sought to restore order by reminding the Corinthians that God had made a difference between men and women, that each had a proper place to God's economy. There were also appropriate customs that symbolized these relationships and reminded both men and women of their correct places in the divine scheme. Paul did not say, or even hint, that *difference* meant *inequality* or *inferiority*. If there is to be peace in the church (1 Cor. 15:33), then there must be some kind of order; and order of necessity involves rank. However, *rank* and *quality* are two different things. The captain has a higher rank than the private, but the private may be a better man.

God's order to the church is based on three fundamentals that Paul considered to be self-evident.

(1) Redemption (vv. 3–7). There is a definite order of "headship" to the church: The Father is the Head over Christ, Christ is the Head of the man, and the man is the head of the woman. Some interpret *head* to mean "origin," but this would mean that the Father originated Christ— something we cannot accept. In His redemptive ministry, the Son was subject to the Father even though He is equal to the Father (John 10:30; 14:28). Likewise, the woman is subject to the man even though to Christ she is equal to the man (1 Cor. 3:21–23; Gal. 3:28; Eph. 5:21–33).

Keep in mind that Paul was writing about the relationship *within the local assembly,* not in the world at large. It is God's plan that in the home and in the local church, the men should exercise headship under the authority of Jesus Christ.

The important fact is this: Both women and men must honor the Lord by respecting the symbols of this headship—hair and the head-covering. Whenever a woman prays or prophesies in the assembly, she must have long hair and must wear a covering. The man should have short hair and not wear any covering. (This would be a change for Paul, for devout Jewish men always wore a cap when they prayed.) The man honors his Head (Christ) by being uncovered, while the woman honors her head (the man) by being covered. She is showing her submission both to God and to the man.

The Corinthian women who appeared in the assembly without the head-covering were actually putting themselves on the low level of the temple prostitutes. The prostitutes wore their hair very short, and they did not wear a head-covering in public. Their hairstyle and manner announced to others just what they were and what they were offering. "If you are going to abandon the covering," wrote Paul, "then why not go all the way and cut your hair?"

In Jewish law, a woman proved guilty of adultery had her hair cut off (Num. 5:11–31). Paul used two different words in 1 Corinthians 11:5–6: *Shaved* means exactly that, all the hair shaved off; *shorn* means "cut short." Either one would be a disgrace to a woman.

Both man and woman are made in the image of God and for the glory of God; but since the woman was made from the man (Gen. 2:18–25), she is also the "glory of the man." She glorifies God and brings glory to the man by submitting to God's order and keeping her head covered in public worship. Thus, Paul tied together both local custom and biblical truth, the one pointing to the other.

(2) Creation (vv. 8–12). We have already touched briefly on this truth. God's order is based on the fact that man was created first (1 Tim. 2:13), and that the woman was created for the man. Again, priority does not imply inferiority; for Paul made it clear in 1 Corinthians 11:11–12 that there is *partnership* as well as headship in God's creation. The man and the woman are spiritually one in the Lord (Gal. 3:28), and one cannot do without the other. Furthermore, the woman may have come from the man at the beginning, but today, it is the man who is born of the woman. Man and woman belong to each other and need each other.

Why did Paul bring up the angels in 1 Corinthians 11:10? He was arguing from the facts of creation, and the angels were a part of that creation. The angels also know their place and show respect when they worship God, for they cover their faces (Isa. 6:2). Finally, in some special way, the angels share in the public worship of the church and learn from the church (Eph. 3:10; 1 Peter 1:12). Public worship is a serious thing, for the angels are present; and we ought to conduct ourselves *as if we were in heaven.*

(3) Nature (vv. 13–16). In a general way, it is true that nature gives women longer hair and men shorter hair. The Romans, Greeks, and Jews (except for the Nazarites) pretty much followed this custom. Nowhere does the Bible tell us how long our hair should be. It simply states that there ought to be a noticeable difference between the length of the men's hair and the women's hair so that there be no confusion of the sexes. It is shameful for the man to look like a woman or the woman to look like a man.

The woman's long hair is her glory, and it is given to her *"instead of a covering"* (literal translation). In other words, if local custom does not dictate a head-covering, her long hair can be that covering. I do not think that Paul meant for all women in every culture to wear a shawl for a head-covering; but he did expect them to use their long hair as a covering and as a symbol of their submission to God's order. This is something that every woman can do.

In my ministry in different parts of the world, I have noticed that the basic principle of headship applies in every culture; but the means of demonstrating it differs from place to place. The important thing is the submission of the heart to the Lord and the public manifestation of obedience to God's order.

2. Selfishness at the "Love Feasts" (11:17–22)

Since the beginning of the church, it was customary for the believers to eat together (Acts 2:42, 46). It was an opportunity for fellowship and for sharing with those who were less privileged. No doubt they climaxed this meal by observing the Lord's Supper. They called this meal "the love feast" since its main emphasis was showing love for the saints by sharing with one another.

The "agape feast" (from the Greek word for "love") was part of the worship at Corinth, but some serious abuses had crept in. As a result, the love feasts were doing more harm than good to the church. For one thing, there were various cliques in the church, and people ate with their own "crowd" instead of fellowshipping with the whole church family. While Paul condemned this selfish practice, he did take a positive view of the results: At least God would use this to reveal those who were true believers.

Another fault was selfishness: The rich people brought a great deal of food for themselves, while the poorer members went hungry. The original idea of the agape feast was sharing, but that idea had been lost. Some of the members were even getting drunk. It is likely that the weekly agape feast was the only decent meal some of the poorer members regularly had; and to be treated so scornfully by the richer members not only hurt their stomachs, but also their pride.

Of course, the divisions at the dinner were but evidence of the deeper problems in the church. The Corinthians thought they were advanced believers, when in reality they were but little children. Paul did not suggest that they abandon the feast, but rather that they restore its proper meaning. "Let the rich eat at home if they are hungry. When you abuse believers who are less fortunate than you are, then you are actually despising the church!" The agape feast should have been an opportunity for edification, but they were using it as a time for embarrassment.

I recall an incident at a Sunday school picnic when I was just a teenager. The person in charge of the games set up a relay that involved various people throwing eggs to each other as they backed farther and farther apart. Of course, the farther the teams went from each other, the harder the participants had to throw the eggs, and the results were hilarious.

However, some of us noticed two Sunday school children watching the eggs with great fascination. They came from a poor family that probably rarely ate eggs because they could not afford them. The little girl went to the woman leading the games and asked, "If there are any eggs left over, can my brother and I take them home?" Wisely, the woman stopped the game before it was really over, awarded the prizes, and gave all the eggs to the two children. She knew that it was wrong for some of the saints to have a good time at the expense of others.

A drinking party is hardly the best way to prepare for the Lord's Supper. Scorning others is certainly not the way to remember the Savior who died for all sinners, rich and poor. How important it is that we prepare our hearts when we come to the Lord's Table!

3. ABUSES AT THE LORD'S SUPPER (11:23–34)

Evangelical churches recognize two ordinances established by Jesus Christ for His people to observe: baptism and the Lord's Supper. (The Supper is also called *the Communion,* as in 1 Corinthians 10:16, and *the Eucharist,* which means "the giving of thanks.") Jesus Christ took the cup and the loaf—the ingredients of a common meal in that day—and transformed them into a meaningful spiritual experience for believers. However, the value of the experience depends on the condition of the hearts of those who participate; and this was the problem at Corinth.

It is a serious thing to come to the Communion with an unprepared heart. It is also a serious thing to receive the Supper in a careless manner. Because the Corinthians had been sinning in their observing of the Lord's Supper, God had disciplined them. "For this cause many are weak and sickly among you, and many sleep [have died]" (1 Cor. 11:30).

The Lord's Supper gives us an opportunity for spiritual growth and blessings if we approach it in the right attitude. What, then, must we do if the Supper is to bring blessing and not chastening?

First, we should look back (vv. 23–26a). The broken bread reminds us of Christ's body, given for us; and the cup reminds us of His shed blood. It is a remarkable thing that Jesus wants His followers to remember His *death*. Most of us try to forget how those we love died, but Jesus wants us to remember how He died. Why? Because everything we have as Christians centers in that death.

We must remember *that* He died, because this is a part of the gospel message: "Christ died … and … was buried" (1 Cor. 15:3–4). It is not the life of our Lord, or His teachings, that will save sinners—but His death. Therefore, we also remember *why* He died: Christ died for our sins; He was our substitute (Isa. 53:6; 1 Peter 2:24), paying the debt that we could not pay.

We should also remember *how* He died: willingly, meekly, showing forth His love for us (Rom. 5:8). He gave His body into the hands of wicked men, and He bore on His body the sins of the world.

However, this "remembering" is not simply the recalling of historical facts. It is a participation in spiritual realities. At the Lord's Table, we do not walk around a monument and admire it. We have fellowship with a living Savior as our hearts reach out by faith.

Second, we should look ahead (v. 26b). We observe the Supper "till he come." The return of Jesus Christ is the blessed hope of the church and the individual Christian. Jesus not only died for us, but He arose again and ascended to heaven; and one day He shall return to take us to heaven. Today, we are not all that we should be; but when we see Him, "we shall be like him" (1 John 3:2).

Third, we should look within (vv. 27–28, 31–32). Paul did not say that we had to be *worthy* to partake of the Supper, but only that we should partake *in a worthy manner*. At a Communion service in Scotland, the pastor noted that a woman in the congregation did not accept the bread and cup from the elder, but instead sat weeping. The pastor left the table and went to her side and said, "Take it, my dear, *it's for sinners!*" And, indeed, it is; but sinners saved by God's grace must not treat the Supper in a sinful manner.

If we are to participate in a worthy manner, we must examine our own hearts, judge our sins, and confess them to the Lord. To come to the Table with unconfessed sin in our lives is to be guilty of Christ's body and blood, for it was sin that nailed Him to the cross. If we will not judge our own sins, then God will judge us and chasten us until we do confess and forsake our sins.

The Corinthians neglected to examine themselves, but they were experts at examining everybody else. When the church gathers together, we must be careful not to become "religious detectives" who watch others, but who fail to acknowledge our own sins. If we eat and drink in an unworthy manner, we eat and drink judgment (chastening) to ourselves, and that is nothing to take lightly.

Chastening is God's loving way of dealing with His sons and daughters to encourage them to mature (Heb. 12:1–11). It is not a judge condemning a criminal, but a loving Father punishing His disobedient (and perhaps stubborn) children. Chastening proves God's love for us, and chastening can, if we cooperate, perfect God's life in us.

Finally, we should look around (vv. 33–34). We should not look around in order to criticize other believers, but in order to discern the Lord's body (1 Cor. 11:29). This perhaps has a dual meaning: We should discern His body in the loaf, but also in the church around us—for the church is the body of Christ. "For we being many are one bread, and one body" (1 Cor. 10:17). The Supper should be a demonstration of the unity of the church—but there was not much unity in the Corinthian church. In fact, their celebration of the Lord's Supper was only a demonstration of their disunity.

The Lord's Supper is a family meal, and the Lord of the family desires that His children love one another and care for one another. It is impossible for a true Christian to get closer to his Lord while at the same time he is separated from his fellow believers. How can we remember the Lord's death and not love one another? "Beloved, if God so loved us, we ought also to love one another" (1 John 4:11).

No one ought to come to the Table who is not a true believer. Nor should a true believer come to the Table if his heart is not right with God and with his fellow Christians. This is why many churches have a time of spiritual preparation before they observe the Lord's Supper, lest any of the participants bring chastening on themselves. I recall one church member who approached me and shared with me a personal defeat that had not only hurt him spiritually, but had been "advertised" by others and was about to bring reproach on him and the church.

"What can I do to make this right?" he asked, convincing me that he had indeed judged the sin and confessed it. I reminded him that the next week we were going to observe the Lord's Supper, and I suggested that he ask the Lord for direction. The evening of the Supper, I opened the service in a way I had not done before. "Is there anyone here who has anything to share with the church?" I asked, and my repentant friend stood to his feet and walked forward, meeting me at the table. In a quiet, concise manner, he admitted that he had sinned, and he asked the church's forgiveness. We felt a wave of Spirit-given love sweep over the congregation, and people began to weep openly. At that observance of the Supper, we truly discerned the Lord's body.

The Communion is not supposed to be a time of "spiritual autopsy" and grief, even though confession of sin is important. It should be a time of thanksgiving and joyful anticipation of seeing the Lord! Jesus gave thanks, even though He was about to suffer and die. Let us give thanks also.

QUESTIONS FOR PERSONAL REFLECTION
OR GROUP DISCUSSION

1. Why was it so important that the women who were praying and prophesying in the public worship wear head-coverings?

2. Why did Paul warn women against wearing their hair short? How might this principle apply to us today?

3. What was the problem at the "love feasts"? Why was this so upsetting to Paul?

4. How can we be more sensitive to the poor and needy in our churches?

5. What must we do to prepare our hearts for participation in the Lord's Supper?

6. What do we have to look back to during the Lord's Supper (11:23–26)?

7. What are we to look ahead to (11:26)?

8. Paul exhorted believers to examine themselves before partaking of the Lord's Supper. What did he mean? How can someone eat and drink judgment on himself?

9. What does it mean to discern the Lord's body?

10. What in Paul's instructions on the Lord's Supper do you need to take to heart?

Chapter Ten

BE WISE ABOUT THE CHURCH BODY

(1 Corinthians 12—13)

O ne of the marks of an individual's maturity is a growing understanding of, and appreciation for, his own body. There is a parallel in the spiritual life: As we mature in Christ, we gain a better understanding of the church, which is Christ's body. The emphasis in recent years on "body life" has been a good one. It has helped to counteract the wrong emphasis on "individual Christianity" that can lead to isolation from the local church.

Of course, the image of the body is not the only one Paul used in discussing the church, and we must be careful not to press it too far. The church is also a family, an army, a temple, and even a bride; and each image has important lessons to teach us. However, in three of his letters, Paul gave emphasis to the church as a body; and, in each of these passages, he brought out the same three important truths: unity, diversity, and maturity. The following chart makes this clear.

It is impossible to discuss the body without also discussing the ministry of the Holy Spirit. It was the Spirit who gave birth to the body at Pentecost and who ministers in and through the body. In the Corinthian church, unfortunately, the members were grieving the Holy Spirit by the carnal ways in which they were using spiritual gifts. They were like children with toys instead of adults with valuable tools, and they needed to mature.

	Unity	Diversity	Maturity
1 Corinthians	12:1–13	12:14–31	13:1–13
Romans	12:1–5	12:6–8	12:9–21
Ephesians	4:1–6	4:7–12	4:13–16

1. Unity: The Gift of the Spirit (12:1–13)

Since there was division in the Corinthian church, Paul began with an emphasis on the oneness of the church. He pointed out four wonderful bonds of spiritual unity.

(1) We confess the same Lord (vv. 1–3). Paul contrasted their experience as unconverted idolaters with their present experience as Christians. They had worshipped dead idols, but now they belonged to the living God. Their idols never spoke to them, but God spoke to them by His Spirit, and He even spoke *through* them in the gift of prophecy. When they were lost, they were under the control of the demons (1 Cor. 10:20) and were led astray ("carried away," 1 Cor. 12:2). But now the Spirit of God lived in them and directed them.

It is only through the Spirit that a person can *honestly* say, "Jesus is Lord." A sneering sinner may mouth the words, but he is not giving a true confession. (Perhaps Paul was referring to things they had said when influenced by the demons prior to conversion.) It is important to note that the believer is always in control of himself when the Holy Spirit is at work (1 Cor. 14:32) because Jesus Christ *the Lord* is in charge. Any so-called "Spirit manifestation" that robs a person of self-control is not of God; for "the fruit of the Spirit is ... self-control" (Gal. 5:22–23 NASB).

If Jesus Christ truly is Lord in our lives, then there should be unity in the church. Division and dissension among God's people only weakens their united testimony to a lost world (John 17:20–21).

(2) We depend on the same God (vv. 4–6). There is a trinitarian emphasis here: "the same Spirit … the same Lord … the same God." We individually may have different gifts, ministries, and ways of working, but "it is God which worketh in you both to will and to do of his good pleasure" (Phil. 2:13). The source of the gift is God; the sphere for administering the gift is from God; and the energy to use the gift is from God. Why, then, glorify men? Why compete with one another?

(3) We minister to the same body (vv. 7–11). The gifts are given for the good of the whole church. They are not for individual enjoyment, but for corporate employment. The Corinthians especially needed this reminder, because they were using their spiritual gifts selfishly to promote themselves and not to prosper the church. When we accept our gifts with humility, then we use them to promote harmony, and this helps the whole church.

The various gifts are named in 1 Corinthians 12:8–10 and 28, and also in Ephesians 4:11 and Romans 12:6–8. When you combine the lists, you end up with nineteen different gifts and offices. Since the listing in Romans is not identical with the listing in 1 Corinthians, we may assume that Paul was not attempting to exhaust the subject in either passage. While the gifts named are adequate for the ministry of the church, God is not limited to these lists. He may give other gifts as He pleases.

We have already discussed *apostles* (1 Cor. 9:1–6). *Prophets* were New Testament spokesmen for God whose messages came immediately from God by the Spirit. Their ministry was to edify, encourage, and comfort (1 Cor. 14:3). Their messages were tested by the listeners to determine whether they were truly from God (1 Cor. 14:29; 1 Thess. 5:19–21). Ephesians 2:20 makes it clear that apostles and prophets worked together to lay the foundation of the church, and we may assume that they were no longer needed once that foundation was completed.

Teachers (also pastor-teacher) instructed converts in the doctrinal truths of the Christian life. They taught from the Word and from the teachings of the apostles (tradition). Unlike the prophets, they did not get their messages immediately by the Spirit, though the Spirit helped them in their teaching. James 3:1 indicates that this is a serious calling.

The *evangelist* majored on sharing the good news of salvation with the lost. All ministers should do the work of an evangelist (2 Tim. 4:5) and seek to win souls, but some men have been given evangelism as a special calling.

In the early church, *miracles* were a part of the credentials of God's servants (Heb. 2:1–4). In fact, miracles, healings, and tongues all belong to what theologians call "the sign gifts" and belonged in a special way to the infancy of the church. The book of Acts, as well as church history, indicates that these miraculous gifts passed off the scene.

Helps and *governments* have to do with the serving of others and the guiding of the church. Without spiritual leadership, the church flounders. *Ministry* (Rom. 12:7) and *ruling* belong to this same category. In my three pastorates, I was grateful for people with the gifts of helps and leadership.

There were several "speaking gifts": *tongues* and the *interpretation of tongues* (about which more will be said later), the *word of wisdom* and the *word of knowledge* (the ability to understand and apply God's truth to a definite situation), and *exhortation* (encouragement, rebuke if necessary).

Giving and *showing mercy* relate to sharing material aid with those in need, as well as supporting God's servants in ministry. The gift of *faith* has to do with believing God for what He wants to accomplish in the church's ministry, that He will lead and provide. The *discerning of spirits* was important in the early church, since Satan tried to counterfeit the work of God and the Word of God. Today, the Spirit especially uses the written Word to give us discernment (1 John 2:18–24; 4:1–6). Since there are no prophets in the church today, we need not worry about false prophets; but we do have to beware of false *teachers* (2 Peter 2:1).

Some students have categorized the various gifts as the speaking gifts, the sign gifts, and the serving gifts. However, we should not be so fascinated by the individual gifts that we forget the main reason why Paul listed them: to remind us that they unite us in our ministries to the one body. The Holy Spirit bestows these gifts "as he will" (1 Cor. 12:11), not as we will. No Christian should complain about his or her gifts, nor should any believer boast about his or her gifts. We are many members in one body, ministering to each other.

(4) We have experienced the same baptism (vv. 12–13). It is unfortunate that the term "baptism of the Spirit" has been divorced from its original New Testament meaning. God has spoken to us in Spirit-given *words* that we must not confuse (1 Cor. 2:12–13). The baptism of the Spirit occurs at conversion when the Spirit enters the believing sinner, gives him new life, and makes his body the temple of God. *All* believers have experienced this once-for-all baptism (1 Cor. 12:13). Nowhere does the Scripture command us to *seek* this baptism, because we have already experienced it and it need not be repeated.

The "filling of the Spirit" (Eph. 5:18ff.) has to do with the Spirit's control of our lives. (In Scripture, to be *filled by* something means "to be controlled by.") We are *commanded* to be filled, and we can be if we yield all to Christ and ask Him for the Spirit's filling. This is a repeated experience, for we constantly need to be filled with spiritual power if we are to glorify Christ. To be baptized by the Spirit means that we belong to *Christ's body*. To be filled with the Spirit means that *our bodies* belong to Christ.

The evidence of the Spirit's baptism at conversion is the witness of the Spirit within (Rom. 8:14–16). It is not "speaking in tongues." *All* of the believers in the Corinthian assembly had been baptized by the Spirit, but not all of them spoke in tongues (1 Cor. 12:30). The evidences of the Spirit's filling are power for witnessing (Acts 1:8), joyfulness and submission (Eph. 5:19ff.), Christlikeness (Gal. 5:22–26), and a growing understanding of the Word (John 16:12–15).

Because of the gift of the Spirit, which is received at conversion, we are all members of the body of Christ. Race, social status, wealth, or even sex (Gal. 3:28) are neither advantages nor handicaps as we fellowship and serve the Lord.

2. DIVERSITY: THE GIFTS OF THE SPIRIT (12:14–31)

Unity without diversity would produce uniformity, and uniformity tends to produce death. Life is a balance between unity and diversity. As a human body weakens, its systems slow down and everything tends to become uniform. The ultimate, of course, is that the body itself turns to dust.

This helps to explain why some churches (and other Christian ministries) have weakened and died: There was not sufficient diversity to keep unity from becoming uniformity. Dr. Vance Havner has expressed it: "First there is a man, then a movement, then a machine, and then a monument." Many ministries that began as a protest against "dead orthodoxy" became dead themselves, because in their desire to remain pure and doctrinally sound, they stifled creativity and new ideas.

However, if diversity is not kept under control, it could destroy unity; and then you have anarchy. We shall discover in 1 Corinthians 13 that it is *maturity* that balances unity and diversity. The tension in the body between individual members and the total organism can only be solved by maturity.

Using the human body as his illustration, Paul explained three important facts about diversity in the body of Christ. Why are there different members?

(1) The body needs different functions if it is to live, grow, and serve (vv. 14–20). No member should compare or contrast itself with any other member, because each one is different and each one is important. I suppose I could learn to walk on my hands, but I prefer to use my feet, even though I have not yet learned to type or to eat with my feet. The ear cannot see and the eye cannot hear, yet each organ has an important ministry. And have you ever tried to smell through your ears?

There is a tendency today for some people to magnify the "sensational" gifts. Some believers feel very guilty because they possess gifts that do not put them into the limelight. It is this attitude that Paul opposed and refuted in this paragraph. Diversity does not suggest inferiority. Are we to believe that the sovereign Lord made a mistake when He bestowed the gifts?

(2) The members promote unity as they discover their dependence on one another (vv. 21–26). Diversity in the body is an evidence of the wisdom of God. Each member needs the other members, and no member can afford to become independent. When a part of the human body becomes independent, you have a serious problem that could lead to sickness and even death. In a healthy human body, the various members cooperate with each other and even compensate for each other when a crisis occurs. The instant any part of the body says to any other part, "I don't need you!" it begins to weaken and die and create problems for the whole body.

A famous preacher was speaking at a ministers' meeting, and he took time before and after the meeting to shake hands with the pastors and chat with them. A friend asked him, "Why take time for a group of men you may never see again?" The world-renowned preacher smiled and said, "Well, I may be where I am because of them! Anyway, if I didn't need them on the way up, I might need them on the way down!" No Christian servant can say to any other servant, "My ministry can get along without you!"

Paul may be referring to the private parts of the body in 1 Corinthians 12:23–24. If so, then to "bestow honor" on them refers to the use of attractive clothing. The more beautiful parts of the body need no special help.

God's desire is that there be no division ("schism") in the church. Diversity leads to disunity when the members compete with one another; but diversity leads to unity when the members care for one another. How do the members care for each other? By each one functioning according to God's will and helping the other members to function. If one member suffers, it affects every member. If one member is healthy, it helps the others to be strong.

(3) Diversity of members fulfills the will of God in the body (vv. 27–31). It is God who bestows the gifts and assigns the offices. He has a perfect plan, not only for the church as a whole, but also for each local congregation. We have no reason to believe that each congregation in the New Testament possessed all of the gifts. The church at Corinth was an especially gifted assembly (1 Cor. 1:4–7; 2 Cor. 8:7). However, God gives to each congregation just the gifts it needs when they are needed.

In this paragraph, Paul pointed out that there is a "priority list" for the gifts, that some have more significance than others. But this fact does not contradict the lesson already shared—that each gift is important and each individual believer is important. Even in the human body, there are some parts that we can do without, even though their absence might handicap us a bit.

The apostles and prophets, of course, appeared first on the scene because they had a foundational ministry (Eph. 2:20). Teachers were needed to help establish believers in the faith. The other gifts were needed from time to time to help individual believers and to build the church.

The construction of the Greek in 1 Corinthians 12:29–30 demands *no* as the answer to each of these questions. No individual believer possesses all the spiritual gifts. Each believer has the gift (or gifts) assigned to him by the Lord and needed at that time.

The word translated "best" in 1 Corinthians 12:31 simply means "greater." Some spiritual gifts are greater in significance than others, and it is proper for the believer to desire these gifts (1 Cor. 14:1). Paul put a high value on prophecy, but the Corinthians valued the gift of tongues. Paul put tongues at the end of the list.

Unity and diversity must be balanced by maturity, and that maturity comes with love. It is not enough to have the *gift* of the Spirit and *gifts* from the Spirit. We must also have the *graces* of the Spirit as we use our gifts to serve one another.

3. Maturity: The Graces of the Spirit (13:1–13)

It was Jonathan Swift, the satirical author of *Gulliver's Travels,* who said, "We have just enough religion to make us hate, but not enough to make us love one another." Spiritual gifts, no matter how exciting and wonderful, are useless and even destructive if they are not ministered in love. In all three of the "body" passages in Paul's letters, there is an emphasis on love. The main evidence of maturity in the Christian life is a growing love for God and for God's people, as well as a love for lost souls. It has well been said that love is the "circulatory system" of the body of Christ.

Few chapters in the Bible have suffered more misinterpretation and misapplication than 1 Corinthians 13. Divorced from its context, it becomes "a hymn to love" or a sentimental sermon on Christian brotherhood. Many people fail to see that Paul was still dealing with the Corinthians' problems when he wrote these words: the abuse of the gift of tongues, division in the church, envy of others' gifts, selfishness (remember the lawsuits?), impatience with one another in the public meetings, and behavior that was disgracing the Lord.

The only way spiritual gifts can be used creatively is when Christians are motivated by love. Paul explained three characteristics of Christian love that show why it is so important in ministry.

(1) Love is enriching (vv. 1–3). Paul named five spiritual gifts: tongues, prophecy, knowledge, faith, and giving (sacrifice). He pointed out that, without love, the exercise of these gifts is *nothing.* Tongues apart from love is just a lot of noise! It is love that enriches the gift and that gives it value. Ministry without love cheapens both the minister and those who are touched by it; but ministry with love enriches the whole church. "Speaking the truth in love" (Eph. 4:15).

Christians are "taught of God to love one another" (1 Thess. 4:9). God the Father taught us to love by sending His Son (1 John 4:19), and God the Son taught us to love by giving His life and by commanding us to love each other (John 13:34–35). The Holy Spirit teaches us to love one another by pouring out God's love in our hearts (Rom. 5:5). The most important lesson in the school of faith is to love one another. Love enriches all that it touches.

(2) Love is edifying (vv. 4–7). "Knowledge puffeth up, but charity edifieth [builds up]" (1 Cor. 8:1). The purpose of spiritual gifts is the edification of the church (1 Cor. 12:7; 14:3, 5, 12, 17, 26). This means we must not think of ourselves, but of others; and this demands love.

The Corinthians were impatient in the public meetings (1 Cor. 14:29–32), but love would make them long-suffering. They were envying each other's gifts, but love would remove that envy. They were "puffed up" with pride (1 Cor. 4:6, 18–19; 5:2), but love would remove pride and self-vaunting and replace it with a desire to promote others. "Be kindly affectioned one to another with brotherly love; in honour preferring one another" (Rom. 12:10).

At the "love feast" and the Lord's Table, the Corinthians were behaving in a very unseemly manner. If they had known the meaning of real love, they would have behaved themselves in a manner pleasing to the Lord. They were even suing one another! But love "seeketh not [its] own, is not easily provoked, thinketh no evil" (1 Cor. 13:5). The phrase *thinketh no evil* means "does not keep any record of wrongs." One of the most miserable men I ever met was a professed Christian who actually kept in a notebook a list of the wrongs he felt others had committed against him. Forgiveness means that we wipe the record clean and never hold things against people (Eph. 4:26, 32).

Love does not rejoice in iniquity, yet the Corinthians were boasting about sin in their church (1 Cor. 5). Love "shall cover the multitude of sins" (1 Peter 4:8). Like Noah's sons, we should seek to hide the sins of others, and then help them make things right (Gen. 9:20–23).

Read 1 Corinthians 13:4–7 carefully and compare this with the fruit of the Spirit listed in Galatians 5:22–23. You will see that all of the characteristics of love show up in that fruit. This is why love edifies: It releases the power of the Spirit in our lives and churches.

(3) Love is enduring (vv. 8–13). Prophecy, knowledge, and tongues were not permanent gifts. (*Knowledge* does not mean "education," but the immediate imparting of spiritual truth to the mind.) These three gifts went together. God would impart knowledge to the prophet, and he would give the message in a tongue. Then an interpreter (sometimes the prophet himself) would explain the message. These were gifts that some of the Corinthians prized, especially the gift of tongues.

These gifts will fail (be abolished) and cease, but love will endure forever; for "God is love" (1 John 4:8, 16). The Corinthians were like children playing with toys that would one day disappear. You expect a child to think, understand, and speak like a child; but you also expect the child to mature and start thinking and speaking like an adult. The day comes when he must "put away childish things" (1 Cor. 13:11).

In the New Testament (which at that time was not completed) we have a complete revelation, but our understanding of it is partial. (Review 1 Corinthians 8:1–3 if you think otherwise.) There is a maturing process for the church as a whole (Eph. 4:11–16) and also for the individual believer (1 Cor. 14:20; 2 Peter 3:18). We will not be fully completed until Jesus returns, but we ought to be growing and maturing now. Children live for the temporary; adults live for the permanent. Love is enduring, and what it produces will endure.

Note that all three of the Christian graces will endure, even though "faith will become sight and hope will be fulfilled." But the greatest of these graces is love; because when you love someone, you will trust him and will always be anticipating new joys. Faith, hope, and love go together, but it is love that energizes faith and hope.

Unfortunately, some of the emphasis today on the Holy Spirit has not been *holy* (because it has ignored Scripture) and has not been *spiritual* (because it has appealed to the carnal nature). We must not tell other believers what gifts they should have or how they can obtain them. This matter is in the sovereign will of God. We must not minimize gifts, but neither should we neglect the *graces* of the Spirit. In my itinerant ministry, I have run across too many local church problems created by people who were zealous for the gifts, but careless of the graces.

Unity—diversity—maturity; and maturity comes through love.

QUESTIONS FOR PERSONAL REFLECTION
OR GROUP DISCUSSION

1. Why do we sometimes avoid working with certain people in the church? According to 1 Corinthians 12:1–13, what reasons do we have to work together?

2. What is God's purpose in giving Christians spiritual gifts?

3. How have you seen people using their spiritual gifts in your local church body?

4. What are some evidences of the filling of the Spirit?

5. How does the human body demonstrate diversity?

6. What kind of diversity is there among members of your group?

7. How can we keep our diversity from becoming disunity?

8. Why is prophecy or preaching worthless without love?

9. Choose one of the qualities of love that Paul lists in 13:4–7 and explain why it is essential to have when we minister.

10. Which of these qualities of maturity would you most like to grow in?

Chapter Eleven

BE WISE ABOUT USING SPIRITUAL GIFTS

(1 Corinthians 14)

Paul had discussed the gift of the Spirit, the gifts of the Spirit, and the graces of the Spirit; and now he concluded this section by explaining the government of the Spirit in the public worship services of the church. Apparently there was a tendency for some of the Corinthians to lose control of themselves as they exercised their gifts, and Paul had to remind them of the fundamental principles that ought to govern the public meetings of the church. There are three principles: edification, understanding, and order.

1. EDIFICATION (14:1–5, 26B)

This was one of Paul's favorite words, borrowed, of course, from architecture. *To edify* means "to build up." This concept is not alien to the "body" image of the church; even today, we speak about "bodybuilding exercises." There is an overlapping of images here, for the body of Christ is also the temple of the living God. Paul's choice of the word *edify* was a wise one.

The mistake the Corinthians were making was to emphasize their own personal edification to the neglect of the church. They wanted to build themselves up, but they did not want to build up their fellow believers.

This attitude, of course, not only hurt the other Christians, but it also hurt the believers who were practicing it. After all, if we are all members of the same body, the way we relate to the other members must ultimately affect us personally. "The eye cannot say unto the hand, I have no need of thee" (1 Cor. 12:21). If one member of the body is weak or infected, it will affect the other members.

Paul detected that the church was neglecting prophecy and giving a wrong emphasis to tongues. We must not think of a New Testament prophet as a person who foretold the future, for even the Old Testament prophets did more than that. Prophets received God's message immediately, through the Holy Spirit, and communicated that message to the church, usually in a tongue, but not always. Prophecy was not the same as our modern-day "preaching," because today's preachers study the Bible and prepare their messages. No preacher today should claim that he has immediate inspiration from God.

Paul explained the supreme value of prophecy over tongues by contrasting the two gifts.

(1) Prophecy speaks to men, tongues to God (vv. 1–3). "If you are zealous for spiritual gifts, at least desire the best gifts," was Paul's counsel. Prophecy was best because it built up the church. It gave the listeners encouragement and comfort—something that everybody needs.

It is unfortunate that our translators inserted *unknown* in 1 Corinthians 14:2, because the New Testament knows nothing of an "unknown tongue." From the very beginning of the church, tongues were *known* languages, recognized by the listeners (Acts 2:4, 6, 8, 11). The tongue would be unknown *to the speaker* and to the listeners, but it was not unknown in the world (1 Cor. 14:10–11, 21).

It is also unfortunate that people have the idea that tongues were used to preach the gospel to the lost. Quite the contrary was true: Paul was afraid that the excessive tongues-speaking in the church would convince the lost that the Christians were crazy (1 Cor. 14:23)! At Pentecost, the believers extolled "the wonderful works of God," but Peter preached the gospel in the Aramaic language his listeners could all understand.

The believer who speaks in a tongue speaks to God in praise and worship; but the believer who prophesies shares the Word with the church and helps those who listen. This leads to the second contrast.

(2) Prophecy edifies the church, tongues edify only the speaker (vv. 4–5). Paul did not deny the value of tongues to the speaker, but he did place a greater value on building up the church. "Greater is he that prophesieth than he that speaketh with tongues" (1 Cor. 14:5). Unless the tongues are interpreted (1 Cor. 12:10, 30), the message can do the church no good. Paul pointed out that an interpreter must be present before the gift of tongues may be exercised (1 Cor. 14:28).

Keep in mind that the members of the Corinthian church did not sit in the services with Bibles on their laps. The New Testament was being written, and the Old Testament scrolls were expensive and not available to most believers. God spoke to His people directly through the prophets, and the message was sometimes given in a tongue. The three gifts of knowledge, prophecy, and tongues worked together to convey truth to the people (1 Cor. 13:1–2, 8–11).

Paul emphasized the importance of doctrinal teaching in the church. Our worship must be based on truth, or it may become superstitious emotionalism. Christians need to know what they believe and why they believe it. The prophet shared truth with the church, and thereby edified the assembly. The person speaking in tongues (unless there is an interpreter) is enjoying his worship of God, but he is not edifying the church.

In my own ministry, I have shared in many local church services and conferences, and I have always tried to communicate biblical truth to the people. Sometimes the music has not been edifying, and at other times, the music communicated the Word of God in a powerful way. Whenever all of us as ministers have aimed at edification, and not entertainment, God has blessed and the people have been helped. A ministry that does not build up will tear down, no matter how "spiritual" it may seem. When we explain and apply the Word of God to individual lives, we have a ministry of edification.

2. UNDERSTANDING (14:6–25)

Eight times in this section, Paul used the word *understanding*. It is not enough for the minister to impart information to people; the people must *receive* it if it is to do them any good. The seed that is received in the good ground is the seed that bears fruit, but this means that there must be an *understanding* of the Word of God (Matt. 13:23). If a believer wants to be edified, he must prepare his heart to receive the Word (1 Thess. 2:13). Not everybody who *listens* really *hears*.

The famous Congregationalist minister Dr. Joseph Parker preached at an important meeting and afterward was approached by a man who pointed out an error in the sermon. Parker listened patiently to the man's criticism, and then asked, "And what *else* did you get from the message?" This remark simply withered the critic, who then disappeared into the crowd. Too often we are quick to judge the sermon instead of allowing the Word of God to judge us.

Illustration (vv. 6–11). Paul used three simple illustrations to prove his point that there must be understanding if there is to be an edifying spiritual ministry: musical instruments, a bugle call in battle, and daily conversation.

If a musical instrument does not give a clear and distinct sound, nobody will recognize the music being played. Everyone knows how uncomfortable one feels when a performer *almost* plays the right note because the instrument is defective or out of tune. Large pipe organs must be constantly serviced lest their reeds fail to perform properly. I was in a church service one evening during which the organ pitch gradually changed because of atmospheric conditions, and by the close of the service, the organ could not be played with the piano because of the radical change that had occurred.

If the bugler is not sure whether he is calling "Retreat!" or "Charge!" you can be sure none of the soldiers will know what to do either. Half of them will rush forward, while the other half will run back! The call must be a clear one if it is to be understood.

But this fact is also true in everyday conversation. I recall the first time my wife and I visited Great Britain and were confronted with the variety of local dialects there. We asked directions of a friendly gentleman in London and, quite frankly, could understand very little of what he said. (Perhaps he had a difficult time understanding us!)

First Corinthians 14:10 gives us good reason to believe that, when Paul wrote about tongues, he was referring to known languages and not some "heavenly" language. Each language is different and yet each language has its own meaning. No matter how sincere a speaker may be, if I do not understand his language, he cannot communicate with me. To the Greeks, a *barbarian* was the lowest person on the social or national ladder. In fact, anybody who was not a Greek was considered a barbarian.

The musician, the bugler, and the everyday conversationalist cannot be understood unless their messages are communicated in a manner that is meaningful to the listener. Having illustrated the principle of understanding, Paul then applied it to three different persons.

Application (vv. 12–25). Paul first applied the principle of understanding to the speaker himself (1 Cor. 14:12–15). Again, he reminded the Corinthians that it is better to be a blessing to the church than to experience some kind of personal "spiritual excitement." If the believer speaks in a tongue, his spirit (inner person) may share in the experience, but his mind is not a part of the experience. It is not wrong to pray or sing "in the spirit," but it is better to include the mind and understand what you are praying or singing. (Note that the word *spirit* in 1 Corinthians 14:14–15 does not refer to the Holy Spirit, but to the inner person, as in 1 Corinthians 2:11.) If the speaker is to be edified, he must understand what he is saying.

What, then, is the speaker to do? He must ask God for the interpretation of the message. Paul assumed that an interpreter would be present (1 Cor. 14:27–28) or that the speaker himself had the gift of interpreting. Of course, all of this discussion emphasized once again the superiority of prophecy over tongues: prophecy needs no interpretation and can therefore be a blessing to everybody.

Paul then applied the principle to other believers in the assembly (1 Cor. 14:16–20). He assumed that they would listen to the message and respond to it. But if they did not understand the message, how could they respond? (Apparently, saying *Amen!* in church was not frowned on in those days.) The "unlearned" person was probably a new believer, or possibly an interested "seeker." He could not be edified unless he understood what was being said.

Again, it was a matter of priorities. While Paul did not oppose the ministry of tongues, he did try to put it into a right perspective. The issue was not quantity of words, but quality of communication. The Corinthians were acting like children playing with toys. When it came to knowing about sin, Paul wanted them to be "babes"; but when it came to spiritual understanding, he wanted them to be mature men (1 Cor. 3:1–4; 13:11–13).

Some people have the idea that speaking in a tongue is an evidence of spiritual maturity, but Paul taught that it is possible to exercise the gift in an unspiritual and immature manner.

Paul's final application was to the unsaved person who happened to come into the assembly during a time of worship (1 Cor. 14:21–25). Paul made here another point for the superiority of prophecy over tongues: A message in tongues (unless interpreted) could never bring conviction to the heart of a lost sinner. In fact, the unsaved person might leave the service before the interpretation was given, thinking that the whole assembly was crazy. Tongues were not used for evangelism, neither at Pentecost nor in the meetings of the early church.

However, tongues did have a "message" for the lost Jews in particular: They were a sign of God's judgment. Paul quoted Isaiah 28:11–12, a reference to the invading Assyrian army whose "barbaric" language the Jews would not understand. The presence of this "tongue" was evidence of God's judgment on the nation. God would rather speak to His people in clear language they could understand, but their repeated sins made this impossible. He *had* spoken to them through His messengers in their own tongue, and the nation would not repent. Now He had to speak in a foreign tongue, and this meant judgment.

As a nation, the Jews were always seeking a sign (Matt. 12:38; 1 Cor. 1:22). At Pentecost, the fact that the apostles spoke in tongues was a sign to the unbelieving Jews who were there celebrating the feast. The miracle of tongues aroused their interest, but it did not convict their hearts. It took Peter's preaching (in Aramaic, which the people all understood) to bring them to the place of conviction and conversion.

The principle of *edification* encourages us to major on sharing the Word of God so that the church will be strengthened and grow. The principle of *understanding* reminds us that what we share must be understood if it is to do any good. The private use of spiritual gifts may edify the user, but it will not edify the church; and Paul admonished us to "excel to the edifying of the church" (1 Cor. 14:12).

But a third principle must be applied: the principle of order.

3. ORDER (14:26–40)

Two statements in this section go together: "Let all things be done unto edifying" (1 Cor. 14:26), and, "Let all things be done decently and in order"

(1 Cor. 14:40). When a building is constructed, there must be a plan, or everything will be in chaos. I know of a church that had terrible problems building their parsonage, until someone discovered that the lumberyard had a different set of plans from that of the contractor. It was no wonder that the materials shipped to the site did not fit into the building!

The Corinthian church was having special problems with disorder in their public meetings (1 Cor. 11:17–23). The reason is not difficult to determine: They were using their spiritual gifts to please themselves and not to help their brethren. The key word was not *edification,* but *exhibition.* If you think that *your* contribution to the service is more important than your brother's contribution, then you will either be impatient until he finishes, or you will interrupt him. Add to this problem the difficulties caused by the "liberated women" in the assembly, and you can understand why the church experienced carnal confusion.

First Corinthians 14:26 gives us a cameo picture of worship in the early church. Each member was invited to participate as the Lord directed. One would want to sing a psalm (Eph. 5:19; Col. 3:16). Another would be led to share a doctrine. Someone might have a revelation that would be given in a tongue and then interpreted. Apart from some kind of God-given order, there could never be edification.

Note that the tongues speakers were the ones causing the most trouble, so Paul addressed himself to them and gave several instructions for the church to obey in their public meetings.

First, speaking and interpreting, along with judging (evaluating the message) must be done in an orderly manner (1 Cor. 14:27–33). There must not be more than three speakers at any one meeting, and each message must be interpreted and evaluated in order. If no interpreter was present, then the tongues speaker must keep silent. Paul's admonitions to the Thessalonian congregation would apply here: "Quench not the Spirit.

Despise not prophesyings. Prove all things; hold fast that which is good" (1 Thess. 5:19–21).

Why were the messages evaluated? To determine whether the speaker had truly communicated the Word of God through the Holy Spirit. It was possible for a speaker, under the control of his own emotions, to imagine that God was speaking to him and through him. It was even possible for Satan to counterfeit a prophetic message (2 Cor. 11:13–14). The listeners would test the message, then, by Old Testament Scriptures, apostolic tradition, and the personal guidance of the Spirit ("discerning of spirits," 1 Cor. 12:10).

If while a person is speaking, God gives a revelation to another person, the speaker must be silent while the new revelation is shared. If God is in charge, there can be no *competition* or *contradiction* in the messages. If, however, the various speakers are "manufacturing" their messages, there will be confusion and contradiction.

When the Holy Spirit is in charge, the various ministers will have self-control; for self-control is one fruit of the Spirit (Gal. 5:23). I once shared a Bible conference with a speaker who had "poor terminal facilities." He often went fifteen to twenty minutes past his deadline, which meant, of course, that I had to condense my messages at the last minute. He excused himself to me by saying, "You know, when the Holy Spirit takes over, you can't worry about clocks!" My reply was to quote 1 Corinthians 14:32: "And the spirits of the prophets are subject to the prophets."

Our own self-control is one of the evidences that the Spirit is indeed at work in the meeting. One of the ministries of the Spirit is to bring order out of chaos (Gen. 1). Confusion comes from Satan, not from God (James 3:13–18). When the Spirit is leading, the participants are able to minister "one by one" so that the total impact of God's message may be received by the church.

How do we apply this instruction to the church today since we do not have New Testament prophets, but we do have the completed Scripture? For one thing, we must use the Word of God to test every message that we hear, asking the Spirit to guide us. There are false teachers in the world and we must beware (2 Peter 2; 1 John 4:1–6). But even true teachers and preachers do not know everything and sometimes make mistakes (1 Cor. 13:9, 12; James 3:1). Each listener must evaluate the message and apply it to his own heart.

Our public meetings today are more formal than those of the early church, so it is not likely that we need to worry about the order of the service. But in our more informal meetings, we need to consider one another and maintain order. I recall being in a testimony meeting where a woman took forty minutes telling a boring experience and, as a result, destroyed the spirit of the meeting.

Evangelist D. L. Moody was leading a service and asked a man to pray. Taking advantage of his opportunity, the man prayed on and on. Sensing that the prayer was killing the meeting instead of blessing it, Moody spoke up and said, "While our brother finishes his prayer, let us sing a hymn!" Those who are in charge of public meetings need to have discernment— and courage.

Second, the women in the meeting were not to speak (1 Cor. 14:34–35). Paul had already permitted the women to pray and prophesy (1 Cor. 11:5), so this instruction must apply to the immediate context of evaluating the prophetic messages. It would appear that the major responsibility for doctrinal purity in the early church rested on the shoulders of the men, the elders in particular (1 Tim. 2:11–12).

The context of this prohibition would indicate that some of the women in the assembly were creating problems by asking questions and perhaps even generating arguments. Paul reminded the married women to be submitted to their husbands and to get their questions answered at home. (We assume that the unmarried women could counsel with the elders or with other men in their own families.) Sad to say, in too many Christian homes today, it is the wife who has to answer the questions for the husband because she is better taught in the Word.

What "law" was Paul referring to in 1 Corinthians 14:34? Probably Genesis 3:16. (The word *law* was a synonym for the Old Testament Scriptures, especially the first five books.) In 1 Corinthians 11, Paul had discussed the relationship of men and women in the church, so there was no need to go into detail.

Third, participants must beware of "new revelations" that go beyond the Word of God (1 Cor. 14:36–40). "To the law and to the testimony: if they speak not according to this word, it is because there is no light in them" (Isa. 8:20). The church had the Old Testament as well as the oral tradition given by the apostles (2 Tim. 2:2), and this was the standard by which all revelations would be tested. We today have the completed Scriptures as well as the accumulated teachings of centuries of church history to help us discern the truth. The historic evangelical creeds, while not inspired, do embody orthodox theology that can direct us.

In these verses, Paul was answering the church member who might say, "We don't need Paul's help! The Spirit speaks to us. We have received new and wonderful revelations from God!" This is a dangerous attitude, because it is the first step toward rejecting God's Word and accepting counterfeit revelations, including the doctrines of demons (1 Tim. 4:1ff.). "The Word did not originate in your congregation!" Paul replied. "One of the marks of a true prophet is his obedience to apostolic teaching." In this statement, Paul claimed that what he wrote was actually inspired Scripture, "the commandments of the Lord" (1 Cor. 14:37).

First Corinthians 14:38 does not suggest that Paul wanted people to remain ignorant; otherwise, he would not have written this letter and answered their questions. The New International Version translates it, "If he ignores this [Paul's apostolic authority], he himself will be ignored [by Paul and the churches]." Fellowship is based on the Word, and those who willfully reject the Word automatically break the fellowship (1 John 2:18–19).

Paul summarized the main teachings of 1 Corinthians 14 in verses 39–40. Prophecy is more important than tongues, but the church should not prohibit the correct exercise of the gift of tongues. The purpose of spiritual gifts is the edification of the whole church, and therefore, gifts must be exercised in an orderly manner. Public worship must be carried on "in a seemly manner," that is, with beauty, order, and spiritual motivation and content.

Before leaving this chapter, it might be helpful to summarize what Paul wrote about the gift of tongues. It is the God-given ability to speak in a known language with which the speaker was not previously acquainted. The purpose was not to win the lost, but to edify the saved. Not every believer had this gift, nor was this gift an evidence of spirituality or the result of a "baptism of the Spirit."

Only three persons were permitted to speak in tongues in any one meeting, and they had to do so in order and with interpretation. If there was no interpreter, they had to keep silent. Prophecy is the superior gift, but tongues were not to be despised if they were exercised according to Scripture.

When the foundational work of the apostles and prophets ended, it would seem that the gifts of knowledge, prophecy, and tongues would no longer be needed. "Whether there be tongues, they shall cease" (1 Cor. 13:8). Certainly God could give this gift today if He pleased, but I am not prepared to believe that every instance of tongues is divinely energized. Nor would I go so far as to say that all instances of tongues are either satanic or self-induced.

It is unfortunate when believers make tongues a test of fellowship or spirituality. That in itself would alert me that the Spirit would not be at work. Let's keep our priorities straight and major on winning the lost and building the church.

QUESTIONS FOR PERSONAL REFLECTION
OR GROUP DISCUSSION

1. What did Paul mean by the term edifying or building up the church?

2. What mistake were the members of the Corinthian church making?

3. How does Paul define speaking in tongues and prophecy? What is their purpose?

4. Why is prophecy the more desirable gift?

5. What part does the mind play in worship?

6. What point is Paul making with the illustration of the trumpeter or bugler (14:8)?

7. What guidelines does Paul give for speaking in tongues? For prophesying? Why?

8. How do we apply today the instruction for women to keep silent in the church?

9. How can we tell when people at a worship meeting are more interested in exhibition than in edification?

10. How can we apply these lessons on church order to our own public worship?

Chapter Twelve

BE WISE ABOUT THE RESURRECTION

(1 Corinthians 15)

C orinth was a Greek city, and the Greeks did not believe in the resurrection of the dead. When Paul had preached at Athens and declared the fact of Christ's resurrection, some of his listeners actually laughed at him (Acts 17:32). Most Greek philosophers considered the human body a prison, and they welcomed death as deliverance from bondage.

This skeptical attitude had somehow invaded the church, and Paul had to face it head-on. The truth of the resurrection had doctrinal and practical implications for life that were too important to ignore. Paul dealt with the subject by answering four basic questions.

1. ARE THE DEAD RAISED? (15:1–19)

It is important to note that the believers at Corinth did believe in the resurrection of Jesus Christ; so Paul started his argument with that fundamental truth. He presented three proofs to assure his readers that Jesus Christ indeed had been raised from the dead.

Proof #1—their salvation (vv. 1–2). Paul had come to Corinth and preached the message of the gospel, and their faith had transformed their lives. But an integral part of the gospel message was the fact of Christ's resurrection. After all, a dead Savior cannot save anybody. Paul's readers had received the Word, trusted Christ, been saved, and were now standing on that Word as the assurance of their salvation. The fact that they were standing firm was proof that their faith was genuine and not empty.

Proof #2—the Old Testament Scriptures (vv. 3–4). *First of all* means "of first importance." The gospel is the most important message that the church ever proclaims. While it is good to be involved in social action and the betterment of mankind, there is no reason why these ministries should preempt the gospel. "Christ died … he was buried … he rose again … he was seen" are the basic historical *facts* on which the gospel stands (1 Cor. 15:3–5). "Christ died *for our sins"* is the theological explanation of the historical facts. Many people were crucified by the Romans, but only one "victim" ever died for the sins of the world.

When Paul wrote "according to the scriptures" (1 Cor. 15:3) he was referring to the Old Testament Scriptures. Much of the sacrificial system in the Old Testament pointed to the sacrifice of Christ as our substitute and Savior. The annual Day of Atonement (Lev. 16) and prophecies like Isaiah 53 would also come to mind.

But where does the Old Testament declare His resurrection on the third day? Jesus pointed to the experience of Jonah (Matt. 12:38–41). Paul also compared Christ's resurrection to the "firstfruits," and the firstfruits were presented to God on the day following the Sabbath after Passover (Lev. 23:9–14; 1 Cor. 15:23). Since the Sabbath must always be the seventh day, the day after Sabbath must be the *first* day of the week, or Sunday, the day of our Lord's resurrection. This covers three days on the Jewish calendar. Apart from the Feast of Firstfruits, there were other prophecies of Messiah's resurrection in the Old Testament: Psalm 16:8–11 (see Acts 2:25–28); Psalm 22:22ff. (see Heb. 2:12); Isaiah 53:10–12; and Psalm 2:7 (see Acts 13:32–33).

Proof #3—Christ was seen by witnesses (vv. 5–11). On the cross, Jesus was exposed to the eyes of unbelievers; but after the resurrection, He was seen by believers who could be witnesses of His resurrection (Acts 1:22; 2:32; 3:15; 5:32). Peter saw Him and so did the disciples collectively. James was a half brother of the Lord who became a believer after the Lord appeared to him (John 7:5; Acts 1:14). The five hundred *plus* brethren all saw Him at the same time (1 Cor. 15:6), so it could not have been a hallucination or a deception. This event may have been just before His ascension (Matt. 28:16ff.).

But one of the greatest witnesses of the resurrection was Paul himself, for as an unbeliever he was soundly convinced that Jesus was dead. The radical change in his life—a change that brought him persecution and suffering—is certainly evidence that the Lord had indeed been raised from the dead. Paul made it clear that his salvation was purely an act of God's grace; but that grace worked in and through him as he served the Lord. "Born out of due time" probably refers to the future salvation of Israel when they, like Paul, see the Messiah in glory (Zech. 12:10—13:6; 1 Tim. 1:16).

At this point, Paul's readers would say, "Yes, we agree that *Jesus* was raised from the dead." Then Paul would reply, "If you believe that, then you must believe in the resurrection of *all* the dead!" Christ came as a man, truly human, and experienced all that we experience, except that He never sinned. If there is no resurrection, then Christ was not raised. If He was not raised, there is no gospel to preach. If there is no gospel, then you have believed in vain and you are still in your sins! If there is no resurrection, then believers who have died have no hope. We shall never see them again!

The conclusion is obvious: Why be a Christian if we have only suffering in this life and no future glory to anticipate? (In 1 Corinthians 15:29–34, Paul expanded this idea.) The resurrection is not just important; it is "of first importance," because all that we believe hinges on it.

2. When Are the Dead Raised? (15:20–28)

Paul used three images to answer this question.

(1) Firstfruits (vv. 20, 23). We have already noted this reference to the Old Testament feast (Lev. 23:9–14). As the Lamb of God, Jesus died on Passover. As the sheaf of firstfruits, He arose from the dead three days later on the first day of the week. When the priest waved the sheaf of the firstfruits before the Lord, it was a sign that the entire harvest belonged to Him. When Jesus was raised from the dead, it was God's assurance to us that we shall also be raised one day as part of that future harvest. To believers, death is only "sleep." The body sleeps, but the soul is at home with the Lord (2 Cor. 5:1–8; Phil. 1:21–23). At the resurrection, the body will be "awakened" and glorified.

(2) Adam (vv. 21–22). Paul saw in Adam a type of Jesus Christ *by the way of contrast* (see also Rom. 5:12–21). The first Adam was made from the earth, but the Last Adam (Christ, 1 Cor. 15:45–47) came from heaven. The first Adam disobeyed God and brought sin and death into the world, but the Last Adam obeyed the Father and brought righteousness and life.

The word *order* in 1 Corinthians 15:23 originally referred to military rank. God has an order, a sequence, in the resurrection. Passages like John 5:25–29 and Revelation 20 indicate that there is no such thing taught in Scripture as a "general resurrection." When Jesus Christ returns in the air, He will take His church to heaven and at that time raise from the dead all who have trusted Him and have died in the faith (1 Thess. 4:13–18). Jesus called this "the resurrection of life" (John 5:29). When Jesus returns to the earth in judgment, then the lost will be raised in "the resurrection of damnation" (John 5:29; Rev. 20:11–15). Nobody in the first resurrection will be lost, but nobody in the second resurrection will be saved.

(3) The kingdom (vv. 24–28). When Jesus Christ comes to the earth to judge, He will banish sin for a thousand years and establish His kingdom (Rev. 20:1–6). Believers will reign with Him and share His glory and authority. This kingdom, prophesied in the Old Testament, is called "the millennium" by prophetic teachers. The word comes from the Latin: *mille*—thousand, *annum*—year.

But even after the millennium, there will be one final rebellion against God (Rev. 20:7–10), which Jesus Christ will put down by His power. The lost will then be raised, judged, and cast into the lake of fire. Then death itself shall be cast into hell, and the last enemy shall be destroyed. Jesus Christ will have put all things under His feet! He will then turn the kingdom over to the Father, and then the eternal state—the new heavens and new earth—shall be ushered in (Rev. 21—22).

Good and godly students of the Word have not always agreed on the details of God's prophetic program, but the major truths seem to be clear. Jesus Christ reigns in heaven today, and all authority is "under his feet" (Ps. 110; Eph. 1:15–23). Satan and man are still able to exercise choice, but God is sovereignly in control. Jesus Christ is enthroned in heaven today (Ps. 2). The resurrection of the saved has not yet taken place, nor the resurrection of the lost (2 Tim. 2:17–18).

When will Jesus Christ return for His church? Nobody knows; but when it occurs, it will be "in a moment, in the twinkling of an eye" (1 Cor. 15:52). It behooves us to be ready (1 John 2:28—3:3).

3. WHY ARE THE DEAD RAISED? (15:29–34, 49–58)

The resurrection of the human body is a future event that has compelling implications for our personal lives. If the resurrection is not true, then we can forget about the future and live as we please! But the resurrection *is* true! Jesus *is* coming again! Even if we die before He comes, we shall be raised at His coming and stand before Him in a glorified body.

Paul cited four areas of Christian experience that are touched by the fact of the resurrection.

(1) Evangelism (v. 29). What does it mean to be "baptized for the dead"? Some take this to mean "proxy baptism," where a believer is baptized on behalf of a dead relative; but we find no such teaching in the New Testament. In the second century, there were some heretical groups that practiced "vicarious baptism," but the church at large has never accepted the practice. To begin with, salvation is a personal matter that each must decide for himself; and, second, nobody needs to be baptized to be saved.

The phrase probably means "baptized to take the place of those who have died." In other words, if there is no resurrection, why bother to witness and win others to Christ? Why reach sinners who are then baptized and take the place of those who have died? If the Christian life is only a "dead-end street," get off of it!

Each responsible person on earth will share in either the resurrection of life and go to heaven, or the resurrection of judgment and go to hell (John 5:28–29). We weep for believers who have died, but we ought also to weep for unbelievers who still have opportunity to be saved! The reality of the resurrection is a motivation for evangelism.

(2) Suffering (vv. 30–32). *I die daily* does not refer to "dying to self," as in Romans 6, but to the physical dangers Paul faced as a servant of Christ (2 Cor. 4:8—5:10; 11:23–28). He was in constant jeopardy from his enemies and on more than one occasion had been close to death. Why endure suffering and danger if death ends it all? "Let us eat and drink; for tomorrow we shall die" (Isa. 22:13).

What we do in the body in this life comes up for review at the judgment seat of Christ (2 Cor. 5:10). God deals with the *whole* person, not just with the "soul." The body shares in salvation (Rom. 8:18–23). The suffering endured in the body will result in glory at the resurrection (2 Cor. 4:7–18). If there is no future for the body, then why suffer and die for the cause of Christ?

(3) Separation from sin (vv. 33–34). If there is no resurrection, then what we do with our bodies will have no bearing on our future. Immorality was a way of life in Corinth, and some of the believers rejected the resurrection in order to rationalize their sin. "Evil company corrupts good morals" is a quotation from the Greek poet Menander, a saying no doubt familiar to Paul's readers. The believer's body is the temple of God and must be kept separated from the sins of the world (2 Cor. 6:14—7:1). To fellowship with the "unfruitful works of darkness" (Eph. 5:6–17) is only to corrupt God's temple.

It was time for the Corinthians to *wake up* and *clean up* (1 Thess. 5:4–11). The believer who is compromising with sin has no witness to the lost around him, those who "have not the knowledge of God." What a shameful thing to be selfishly living in sin while multitudes die without Christ!

(4) Death (vv. 49–57). The heavenly kingdom is not made for the kind of bodies we now have, bodies of flesh and blood. So when Jesus returns, the bodies of living believers will instantly be transformed to be like His body (1 John 3:1–3), and the dead believers shall be raised with new glorified bodies. Our new bodies will not be subject to decay or death.

Sigmund Freud, the founder of psychiatry, wrote, "And finally there is the painful riddle of death, for which no remedy at all has yet been found, nor probably ever will be." Christians have victory *in* death and *over* death! Why? Because of the victory of Jesus Christ in His own resurrection. Jesus said, "Because I live, ye shall live also" (John 14:19).

Sin, death, and the law go together. The law reveals sin, and the "wages of sin is death" (Rom. 6:23). Jesus bore our sins on the cross (1 Peter 2:24), and also bore the curse of the law (Gal. 3:13). It is through Him that we have this victory, and we share the victory *today*. The literal translation of 1 Corinthians 15:57 is, "But thanks be to God who *keeps on giving us the victory* through our Lord Jesus Christ." We experience "the power of his resurrection" in our lives as we yield to Him (Phil. 3:10).

First Corinthians 15:58 is Paul's hymn of praise to the Lord, as well as his closing admonition to the church. Because of the assurance of Christ's victory over death, we know that nothing we do for Him will ever be wasted or lost. We can be steadfast in our service, unmovable in suffering, abounding in ministry to others, because we know our labor is not in vain. First Corinthians

15:58 is the answer to Ecclesiastes, where thirty-eight times Solomon used the sad word *vanity*. "Vanity of vanities, all is vanity!" wept Solomon; but Paul sang a song of victory!

4. How Are the Dead Raised? (15:35–48)

Being philosophers, the Greeks reasoned that the resurrection of the human body was an impossibility. After all, when the body turned to dust, it became soil from which other bodies derived nourishment. In short, the food that we eat is a part of the elements of the bodies of generations long gone. When the body of the founder of Rhode Island, Roger Williams, was disinterred, it was discovered that the roots of a nearby apple tree had grown through the coffin. To some degree, the people who ate the apples partook of his body. At the resurrection, then, who will claim the various elements?

Paul's reply to this kind of reasoning was very blunt: "You fool!" Then he made the important point that *resurrection is not reconstruction*. Nowhere does the Bible teach that, at the resurrection, God will "put together the pieces" and return to us our former bodies. There is *continuity* (it is *our* body), but there is not *identity* (it is not the *same* body).

Paul knew that such miracles cannot be explained, so he used three analogies to make the doctrine clear.

(1) **Seeds (vv. 35–38, 42–48).** When you sow seed, you do not expect that same seed to come up at the harvest. The seed dies, but from that death there comes life. (See John 12:23–28 for our Lord's use of this same analogy.) You may sow a few grains of wheat, but you will have many grains when the plant matures. Are they the same grains that were planted? No, but there is still continuity. You do not sow wheat and harvest barley.

Furthermore, what comes up at the harvest is usually more beautiful than what was planted. This is especially true of tulips. Few things are as ugly as a tulip bulb, yet it produces a beautiful flower. If at the resurrection, all God did was to put us back together again, there would be no improvement.

Furthermore, flesh and blood cannot inherit God's kingdom. The only way we can enjoy the glory of heaven is to have a body suited to that environment.

Paul discussed the details of this marvelous change in 1 Corinthians 15:42–48. The body is sown (in burial) in corruption, because it is going to decay; but it is raised with such a nature that it cannot decay. There is no decay or death in heaven. It is buried in humility (in spite of the cosmetic skill of the mortician); but it is raised in glory. In burial, the body is weak; but in resurrection, the body has power. We shall be like Jesus Christ!

Today, we have a "natural body," that is, a body suited to an earthly environment. We received this body from our first parent, Adam: He was made of dust, and so are we (Gen. 2:7). But the resurrection body is suited to a spiritual environment. In His resurrection body, Jesus was able to move quickly from place to place, and even walk through locked doors; yet He was also able to eat food, and His disciples were able to touch Him and feel Him (Luke 24:33–43; John 20:19–29).

The point Paul was making was simply this: The resurrection body completes the work of redemption and gives to us the image of the Savior. We are made in the image of God as far as personality is concerned, but in the image of Adam as far as the body is concerned. One day we shall bear the image of the Savior when we share in His glory.

First Corinthians 15:46 states an important biblical principle: first the "natural" (earthly), and then the "spiritual" (heavenly). The first birth gives us that which is natural, but the second birth gives us that which is spiritual. God rejects the first birth, the natural, and says, "You must be born again!" He rejected Cain and chose Abel. He rejected Abraham's firstborn, Ishmael, and chose Isaac, the second-born. He rejected Esau and chose Jacob. If we depend on our first birth, we shall be condemned forever; but if we experience the new birth, we shall be blessed forever.

(2) Flesh (v. 39). Paul anticipated here the discovery of science that the cell structure of different kinds of animals is different; and therefore, you cannot breed various species indiscriminately. The human body has a nature of one kind, while animals, birds, and fish have their own particular kind of flesh. The conclusion is this: If God is able to make different kinds of bodies for men, animals, birds, and fish, why can He not make a different kind of body for us at the resurrection? (Pet lovers take note: Paul did not teach here that animals will be resurrected. He only used them as an example.)

(3) Heavenly bodies (vv. 40–41). Not only are there earthly bodies, but there are also heavenly bodies; and they differ from one another. In fact, the heavenly bodies differ from each other in glory as far as the human eye is concerned. Paul is suggesting here that believer may differ from believer in glory, even though all Christians will have glorified bodies. Every cup in heaven will be filled, but some cups will be bigger than others, because of the faithfulness and sacrifice of those saints when they were on earth.

These illustrations may not answer every question that we have about the resurrection body, but they do give us the assurances that we need. God will give to us a glorified body suited to the new life in heaven. It will be as unlike our present body in quality as the glory of the sun is unlike a mushroom in the cellar. We will use this new body to serve and glorify God for all eternity.

We must remember that this discussion was not written by Paul merely to satisfy the curiosity of believers. He had some practical points to get across, and he made them very clear in 1 Corinthians 15:29–34. If we really believe in the resurrection of the body, then we will use our bodies today to the glory of God (1 Cor. 6:9–14).

Finally, the lost will be given bodies suited to their environment in hell. They will suffer forever in darkness and pain (Matt. 25:41; 2 Thess. 1:7–10; Rev. 20:11–15). It behooves us who are saved to seek to rescue them from judgment! "Knowing therefore the terror of the Lord, we persuade men" (2 Cor. 5:11).

If you have never trusted the Savior, do so now—before it is too late!

QUESTIONS FOR PERSONAL REFLECTION
OR GROUP DISCUSSION

1. What hope does knowledge of your future resurrection to eternal life give you?

2. How can this resurrection hope enable you to withstand evil and pain in your life?

3. What would be the consequences if we were not going to be raised from the dead?

4. What proofs does Paul use to prove that Jesus Christ really did rise from the dead?

5. Who are the two Adams mentioned in verses 45–49? How are they alike? How are they different? What do they have to do with the resurrection?

6. How does Paul make it clear in verses 35–44 that he is talking about our having bodies, not about our being disembodied souls?

7. What do you learn from 1 Corinthians 15 about what a resurrected body might be like?

8. How does our hope of resurrection affect how we use our current bodies?

9. How does this hope affect our view of death?

10. How does this hope stimulate you to give yourself fully to the Lord's work?

Chapter Thirteen

BE WISE ABOUT CHRISTIAN STEWARDSHIP

(1 Corinthians 16)

It is to the credit of the believers at Corinth that, when they wrote their questions to Paul, they asked him about the collection he was taking for the poor saints in Jerusalem. Paul answered their question and then closed the letter by informing the church of his personal travel plans and also the plans for his associates in the ministry.

This chapter may seem unrelated to our needs today, but actually it deals in a very helpful way with three areas of stewardship: money (1 Cor. 16:1–4), opportunities (1 Cor. 16:5–9), and people (1 Cor. 16:10–24). These are probably the greatest resources the church has today, and they must not be wasted.

1. MONEY (16:1–4)

One of the most important ministries Paul had during his third journey was the gathering of a special "relief offering" for the poor believers in Jerusalem. He wanted to achieve several purposes in this offering. For one thing, the Gentiles owed material help to the Jews in return for the spiritual blessings the Jews had given them (Rom. 15:25–27). At the Jerusalem Conference years before, Paul had agreed to "remember the poor," so he was keeping his pledge (Gal. 2:10). Paul not only preached the gospel, but he also tried to assist those who had physical and material needs.

Why was there such a great need in the Jerusalem church? It is likely that many of the believers had been visiting Jerusalem at Pentecost when they heard the Word and were saved. This meant that they were strangers, without employment, and the church would have to care for them. In the early days of the church, the members had gladly shared with each other (Acts 2:41–47; 4:33–37); but even their resources were limited. There had also been a famine (Acts 11:27–30), and the relief sent at that time could not last for too long a time.

Apart from keeping his promise and meeting a great need, Paul's greatest motive for taking up the offering was to help unite Jewish and Gentile believers. Paul was a missionary to the Gentiles, and this bothered some of the Jewish believers (Acts 17:21–25). Paul hoped that this expression of Gentile love would help to heal some wounds and build some bridges between the churches. (For more information about this offering, read 2 Corinthians 8—9.)

Even though this was a special missionary offering, from Paul's instructions we may learn some basic principles that relate to Christian stewardship.

Giving is an act of worship. Each member was to come to the Lord's Day gathering prepared to give his share for that week. The early church met on the first day of the week in commemoration of the resurrection of Jesus Christ. (The Holy Spirit came on the church at Pentecost on the first day of the week.) It is tragic when church members give only as a duty and forget that our offerings are to be "spiritual sacrifices" presented to the Lord (Phil. 4:18). Giving should be an act of worship to the resurrected and ascended Savior.

Giving should be systematic. Some students have suggested that many people were paid on the first day of the week during that time in history. But even if they were not, each believer was to set aside his offering at home and then bring it to the assembly on the first day. Paul did not want to have to take up a number of collections when he arrived in Corinth. He wanted the whole contribution to be ready. If today's church members were as systematic in their giving as they are in handling their other financial matters, the work of the Lord would not suffer as it sometimes does.

Giving was personal and individual. Paul expected each member to share in the offering, the rich and poor alike. Anyone who had an income was privileged to share and to help those in need. He wanted all to share in the blessing.

Giving is to be proportionate. "As God hath prospered him" (1 Cor. 16:2) suggests that believers who have more should give more. The Jewish believers in the church would have been accustomed to the tithe, but Paul did not mention any special proportion. Certainly the tithe (10 percent of one's income) is a good place to *begin* our stewardship, but we must not remain at that level. As the Lord gives us more, we should plan to give more.

The trouble is, too many saints, as they earn more, involve themselves in more and more financial obligations; and then they do not have more to give to the Lord. Instead of finding a suitable "level" and remaining there, they keep trying to "go higher," and their income is *spent* rather than *invested.* As the old saying goes, "When your outgo exceeds your income, then your upkeep is your downfall."

Paul made it clear in 2 Corinthians 8—9 that Christian giving is a *grace,* the outflow of the grace of God in our lives and not the result of promotion or pressure. An open heart cannot maintain a closed hand. If we appreciate the grace of God extended to us, we will want to express that grace by sharing with others.

Money is to be handled honestly. The various churches involved in this special offering appointed delegates to help Paul manage it and take it safely to Jerusalem. (See 2 Cor. 8:16–24 for more information on the "finance committee" that assisted Paul.) It is unfortunate when Christian ministries lose their testimony because they mismanage funds entrusted to them. Every ministry ought to be businesslike in its financial affairs. Paul was very careful not to allow anything to happen that would give his enemies opportunity to accuse him of stealing funds (2 Cor. 8:20–21).

This explains why Paul encouraged the *churches* to share in the offering and to select dependable representatives to help manage it. Paul was not against *individuals* giving personally; in this chapter, as well as in Romans 16, he named various individuals who assisted him personally. This no doubt included helping him with his financial needs. But generally speaking, Christian giving is church-centered. Many churches encourage their members to give designated gifts through the church budget.

It is interesting that Paul mentioned the offering just after his discussion about the resurrection. There were no "chapter breaks" in the original manuscripts, so the readers would go right from Paul's hymn of victory into his discussion about money. Doctrine and duty go together; so do worship and works. Our giving is "not in vain" because our Lord is alive. It is His resurrection power that motivates us to give and to serve.

2. OPPORTUNITIES (16:5–9)

"Be very careful, then, how you live—not as unwise but as wise, making the most of every opportunity, because the days are evil" (Eph. 5:15–16 NIV). Paul was as careful in his use of time as he was in his use of money. Someone has said that killing time is the chief occupation of modern society, but no Christian can afford to kill time or waste opportunities.

Paul informed his friends at Corinth of his plans for future travel and ministry. It is worth noting that his statements were very tentative: "It may be suitable … it may be … wherever I go … but I trust." Of course, the entire plan was dependent on God's providential leading: "if the Lord permit." Paul's attitude toward his future plans agreed with the injunctions in James 4:13–17.

Paul was at Ephesus when he wrote this letter. His plan was to travel to Macedonia for a time of ministry (*pass through* in 1 Corinthians 16:5 means "travel in a systematic ministry"), winter at Corinth, and then go to Judea with the collection. From November to February, it was impossible to travel by ship; so it would have been convenient for Paul to stay at Corinth and be with his friends. There were some problems to solve in the church, and Paul had promised to come to help the leaders (1 Cor. 11:34).

However, various circumstances forced Paul to revise his plans at least twice. His plan B was to visit Corinth, then travel through Macedonia, passing through Corinth a second time on his way to Judea (2 Cor. 1:15–16). Instead of one long visit, he planned two shorter visits; but even this plan did not materialize. Plan C turned out to be a quick and painful visit to Corinth, after which he returned to Ephesus. He then went to Troas to wait for Titus (who had been sent to Corinth, 2 Cor. 2:12–13; 7:5ff.), visited Macedonia, and then went to Judea. He did not spend as much time at Corinth as he had hoped or as they had expected.

What do we learn from this difficult experience of Paul's? For one thing, a Christian must use his common sense, pray, study the situation, and seek the best he can to determine the will of God. Proverbs 3:5–6 ("lean not unto thine own understanding") must not be interpreted to mean "Put your brain in neutral and don't think!" God gave us our minds and He expects us to think, but He does not want us to *depend* only on our own reasoning. We must pray, meditate on the Word, and even seek the counsel of mature Christian friends.

Second, our decisions may not always be in the will of God. We may make promises that we cannot keep and plans that we cannot fulfill. Does this mean that we are liars or failures? (Some of the believers at Corinth thought Paul was deceptive and not to be trusted. See 2 Cor. 1:12—2:13.) In my own ministry, I have had to change my plans and alter my schedule because of situations over which I had no control. Did this mean I had been out of the will of God in making my plans? Not necessarily. Even an apostle (who had been to heaven and back) occasionally had to revise his datebook.

There are two extremes we must avoid in this important matter of seeking God's will. One is to be so frightened at making a mistake that we make no decisions at all. The other is to make impulsive decisions and rush ahead, without taking time to wait on the Lord. After we have done all we can to determine the leading of the Lord, we must decide and act, and leave the rest to the Lord. If we are in some way out of His will, He will so work that we will finally have His guidance. The important thing is that we sincerely *want* to do His will (John 7:17). After all, He guides us "for his name's sake" (Ps. 23:3), and it is *His* reputation that is at stake.

Paul had an open door of ministry in Ephesus, and this was important to him. He wanted to win the lost in Ephesus, not go to Corinth to pamper the saved. (On "open doors," see Acts 14:27; 2 Cor. 2:12; Col. 4:3; Rev. 3:8.) Paul was neither an optimist nor a pessimist; he was a realist. He saw both the opportunities and the obstacles. God had opened "a great door for effective work," and Paul wanted to seize the opportunities while they were still there.

An ancient Roman proverb says, "While we stop to think, we often miss our opportunity." Once we know what to do, we must do it and not delay. We can usually think of many reasons (or excuses) not to act. Even though Paul was in danger in Ephesus (1 Cor. 15:32), he planned to remain there while the door was open. Like a wise merchant, he had to "buy up the opportunity" before it vanished and would never return.

The stewardship of opportunity is important. The individual believer, and the church family, must constantly ask, *What opportunities is God giving us today?* Instead of complaining about the obstacles, we must take advantage of the opportunities, and leave the results with the Lord.

3. PEOPLE (16:10–24)

Often at the close of his letters, Paul named various people who were a part of his life and his ministry; and what a variety they were! He was not only a soul winner, but he was a friend maker; and many of his friends found their way into dedicated service for the Lord. Evangelist Dwight L. Moody possessed this same gift of making friends and then enlisting them for the Lord's service. Some of the greatest preachers and musicians of the late nineteenth and early twentieth centuries were "found" by Moody, including Ira Sankey, G. Campbell Morgan, Henry Drummond, and F. B. Meyer.

Money and opportunities are valueless without people. The church's greatest asset is people, and yet too often the church takes people for granted. Jesus did not give His disciples money, but He did invest three years training them for service so they might seize the opportunities He would present them. If *people* are prepared, then God will supply both the *opportunities* and the *money* so that His work will be accomplished.

Timothy (vv. 10–11), along with Titus, was one of Paul's special assistants, usually sent to the most difficult places. Timothy had been brought up in a godly home (2 Tim. 1:5), but it was Paul who had led the young man to Christ. Paul usually referred to him as "my own son in the faith" (1 Tim. 1:2). When John Mark abandoned Paul and returned to Jerusalem, it was Timothy who was called to work as Paul's assistant (Acts 16:1–5).

Timothy learned his lessons well and made great progress in Christian life and service (Phil. 2:20–22). Eventually, Timothy took Paul's place at Ephesus, a most difficult place to minister. (It would not be easy to be Paul's successor!) At one point, Timothy wanted to leave the city, but Paul encouraged him to stay (1 Tim. 1:3).

The advice Paul gave the Corinthians about Timothy (1 Cor. 16:10) would suggest that the young man had some physical and emotional problems

(1 Tim. 5:23; 2 Tim. 1:4). He needed all the encouragement he could get. The important thing was that he was doing God's work and laboring with God's servant. A church should not expect every servant of God to be an apostle Paul. Young men starting out in service have great potential, and the church should encourage them. "Let no man despise thee!"

Apollos (vv. 12–14) was an eloquent Jew who was brought into the full understanding of the gospel by Priscilla and Aquila (Acts 18:24–28). He had ministered with great power at Corinth, and there was a segment of the church there that felt attached to him (1 Cor. 1:12; 3:4–8). It is unlikely that Apollos promoted this division, for his great concern seemed to be to preach Christ. In spite of the division ("The Apollos Fan Club"), Paul did not hesitate to encourage Apollos to return to Corinth for further ministry. It is clear that there was no envy on Paul's part or sense of competition on the part of Apollos.

Paul did not have the authority to place men against their will. Apollos did not feel he should go to Corinth at that time, and Paul had to concur with his decision. It is wonderful the way these different men worked together.

Perhaps it was in the light of the divisions in the church that Paul gave the admonitions in 1 Corinthians 16:13–14. *Watch* simply means "Be alert! Be vigilant!" The enemy is always at hand, and we are never safe from attack. Satan would certainly attack the church and try to hinder the ministry of Timothy or Apollos.

To *stand fast in the faith* means to have mature stability. Paul had already warned them that they were immature children who needed to grow up (1 Cor. 3:1ff.). No wonder Paul added, *Quit you like men,* which means, "Act like men, not children." (The word *quit* is short for "acquit"— to perform or act.) It was a call to courageous manliness at an hour when mature leadership was needed.

But even manliness needs to be balanced with love, lest leadership become dictatorship. Paul had expounded the value and virtues of love in 1 Corinthians 13. Carl Sandburg, when addressing the United States Congress, said that Abraham Lincoln was a man of "velvet steel." That is a good image for the Christian to borrow, for true manliness does not exclude tenderness.

Stephanas and his household (vv. 15–18) were the first people to be won to Christ in Achaia, and Paul had baptized them himself, instead of leaving it to one of his helpers (1 Cor. 1:16). They became important leaders in the church, for they "devoted themselves" to Christ's service. The verb means "they appointed themselves," but it does not suggest that they pushed their way into leadership. Rather, whenever they saw a need, they went to work to meet it without waiting to be asked. They were Paul's helpers, and they labored ("toiled to the point of exhaustion") for the Lord. What a wonderful thing it is when an entire family serves the Lord faithfully in the local church.

Stephanas was joined by Fortunatus and Achaicus as an official committee sent from Corinth to Ephesus to confer with Paul about church problems. Paul saw in them a representation of the entire church; their love to Paul compensated for Paul's absence from Corinth. But these men did more than share problems with Paul; they also refreshed his spirit and brought him blessing.

This is a good place to encourage church members to refresh and encourage their pastor. Too often, believers share only problems and burdens with their spiritual leaders, and rarely share the blessings. Who is the pastor's pastor? To whom does the pastor turn for spiritual refreshment and encouragement? Every church member, if he will, can help refresh the pastor and make his burdens lighter.

Paul encouraged the church to honor this very special family and submit to their spiritual leadership. It is right to honor faithful Christians if God gets the glory.

Aquila and Priscilla (vv. 19–20) were a dedicated husband-and-wife team whose lives and ministries intersected and intertwined with Paul's. The apostle met them at Corinth because, like Paul, they were tentmakers (Acts 18:1–3). This godly couple had been expelled from Rome because Aquila was a Jew; but that was only part of God's providence to get them to Corinth where they could assist Paul.

Priscilla must have been a remarkable woman. This couple's names occur in the New Testament six times, and in four of these instances, Priscilla's name stands first. (The best texts put Priscilla first in Acts 18:26.) We get the impression that she was the stronger of the two, a devoted leader and witness. They worked together in serving the Lord and helping Paul.

When Paul moved from Corinth to Ephesus, Aquila and Priscilla packed up and moved their business with him and assisted in founding the church in that needy city (Acts 18:18ff.). So capable were they that Paul left them to oversee the ministry while he returned to Antioch. It was while they were at Ephesus that they assisted Apollos in better understanding the truth of the gospel.

Every local church can be thankful for husbands and wives like Aquila and Priscilla, people who work together in serving the Lord and helping the preacher. The fact that his wife was a better leader did not hinder Aquila from standing with her in their united ministry. (I am sure that Priscilla submitted to her husband and did not try to act important.) One of the Ephesian assemblies met in their house, which shows they were people given to hospitality. Romans 16:4 states that, at one time, this dedicated couple risked their own lives to help save Paul. (See Acts 19:29–30; 20:19 for possible situations where this rescue might have occurred.)

But Priscilla and Aquila did not remain in Ephesus; for when Paul wrote to the saints at Rome, he greeted this couple there (Rom. 16:3). Once again, they had a church meeting in their house (Rom. 16:5). In my itinerant ministry, I have more than once preached to an assembly that had been founded in somebody's living room.

In Paul's last letter, he sent greetings to Prisca (alternate spelling) and Aquila by way of Timothy, who was then overseeing the work in Ephesus (2 Tim. 4:19). This remarkable couple had left Rome and were now back in Ephesus, this time to assist Timothy as they had assisted Paul.

How many couples today would move as often as did Priscilla and Aquila, just to be able to serve the Lord better? And whenever they moved, they had to move their business as well. People with this kind of dedication and sacrifice are not easy to find, but they are great assets to the local church.

Paul's closing words need not detain us. The "holy kiss" (1 Cor. 16:20) was a common mode of greeting, the men kissing the men and the women kissing the women (Rom. 16:16; 2 Cor. 13:12; 1 Thess. 5:26; 1 Peter 5:14). If Paul were writing to Western churches, he would say, "Shake hands with one another."

Paul usually dictated his letters and then took the pen and added his signature. He also added his "benediction of grace" as a mark that the letter was authentic (Gal. 6:11; 2 Thess. 3:17).

The word *anathema* is Aramaic and means "accursed" (1 Cor. 12:3). Not to love Christ means not to believe in Him, and unbelievers are accursed (John 3:16–21). The word *maranatha* is Greek and means "our Lord comes" or (as a prayer) "our Lord, come!" (Rev. 22:20). If a person loves Jesus Christ, he will also love His appearing (2 Tim. 4:8).

Paul had been stern with the Corinthian believers, but he closed his letter by assuring them of his love. After all, "faithful are the wounds of a friend" (Prov. 27:6).

Paul has shared a great deal of spiritual wisdom with us. May we receive it with meekness and put it into practice to the glory of God!

QUESTIONS FOR PERSONAL REFLECTION
OR GROUP DISCUSSION

1. What are some of the struggles we may have when it comes to giving money for God's work?

2. What were Paul's motives for taking up the offering for the Jewish believers in Jerusalem?

3. In what ways is giving money an act of worship?

4. What's the value of giving systematically?

5. How do Paul's methods compare with modern practices of raising support?

6. What can we learn about God's will from the revisions of Paul's travel plans? What extremes must we avoid in seeking God's will?

7. What opportunities for ministry has God given you today?

8. What was Timothy's part in Paul's work? Given what you have learned about the Corinthians, what might Timothy have had to fear (16:10) when he visited those people?

9. In 16:13–14, Paul speaks of the need for both courage and love. Which is the greater challenge for you? Why is that?

10. What will you take away from this study of 1 Corinthians?

The "BE" series . . .

For years pastors and lay leaders have embraced Warren W. Wiersbe's very accessible commentary of the Bible through the individual "BE" series. Through the work of David C. Cook Global Mission, the "BE" series is part of a library of books made available to indigenous Christian workers. These are men and women who are called by God to grow the kingdom through their work with the local church worldwide. Here are a few of their remarks as to how Dr. Wiersbe's writings have benefited their ministry.

"Most Christian books I see are priced too high for me . . .
I received a collection that included 12 Wiersbe
commentaries a few months ago and I have
read every one of them.
I use them for my personal devotions every day and they
are incredibly helpful for preparing sermons.
The contribution David C. Cook is making to the
church in India is amazing."
—Pastor E. M. Abraham, Hyderabad, India

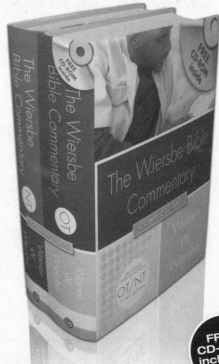